Prayer Solutions

*Biblical Answers to Questions
People Ask About Prayer*

By Dale A. Robbins, D.Min.

Victorious Publications
Grass Valley, California – Nashville, Tennessee
www.victorious.org

Prayer Solutions
Copyright © 2017 Dale A. Robbins
Published by Victorious Publications
Grass Valley, California – Nashville, Tennessee
www.victorious.org

ISBN-10: 0964802244
ISBN-13: 978-0964802247

CONTENTS

Dedicated to our little darlings, Logan and Maddie. Of course you're too small now to read or understand what Papaw has written here. But I thought much about you and your future as I composed these pages, hoping that you will someday read these things, and remember our special times of prayer together, and the faith that Nanna and I sought to instill in your hearts. Trust and follow the Lord Jesus always with your lives, and before long we'll see you again, as we wait to greet and hug you at Heaven's gates!

INTRODUCTION

Before founding the International Prayer Network back in the 1990's, I couldn't have imagined the many thousands of prayer requests we would eventually receive from people around the world. Nor could I have predicted the broad range of questions we would be asked about prayer. While not possible to list them all, this book is a collection of some of those most common inquiries, along with my answers from scripture and personal experience.

As you'll discover, the topics will cover a broad range, from the simple to more complex... but the primary goal is to assure the reader that God still hears and answers prayer. "Prayer Solutions" is what the Lord brings about when people pray. He hears the appeal of those who love and serve Him, and responds with His help... to solve problems, provide guidance and bring solutions for every need.

Thus, please open your heart to the Holy Spirit as you read. My hope and prayer is that the Lord will use this writing to bring encouragement, answers to your questions, and added strength to your faith.

"The Lord says, I will rescue those who love me. I will protect those who trust in my name. When they call on me, I will answer; I will be with them in trouble. I will rescue and honor them" (Psalms 91:14-15 NLT).

1. What Good Does it Do to Pray?

Whenever I am asked about the value of prayer, I often point out the remarks of the Lord's servant, Job... one of His most devoted followers, whose faith was tested to the limits of his endurance. In *Job 21:15, h*e said, *"Who is the Almighty, that we should serve Him? And what profit do we have if we pray to Him?"*

This wasn't an expression of Job's doubts in God's ability to answer prayer. Rather, this was a rhetorical question, responding to the cynicism of those who questioned the value of serving his God. *"Who is God? Why should we obey Him? What good will it do us to pray to God?"*

Job was a person who believed in the Lord intensely, deeply aware of His great power and faithfulness to hear and respond to those who pray. His declaration was to explain the significance of praying to the almighty God of the universe, whose unlimited power can change everything.

These same assurances are repeated throughout scripture, such as in the many teachings of Jesus. He emphasized repeatedly that prayer can have enormous rewards, and taught that praying in faith could acquire the promises of God. In *Matthew 7:7-8, Jesus* said, *"Ask, and it will be given to you; seek, and you will find; knock, and it will be opened to you. For everyone who asks receives, and he who seeks finds, and to him who knocks it will be opened."*

When I was a child, I was always fascinated by the variety of antique photos and items that decorated the walls of grandma's farmhouse. One item I especially remember

1

was a small decoupage with fancy lettering that hung above her couch. I never understood what it meant until I got old enough to read, then always found comfort whenever I would see it. It displayed only three words, a familiar theme that was repeated over and again in her life and with our family. It said, *"Prayer Changes Things."* I eventually came to know this to be a fact, not only because of the words on grandma's wall, nor merely because I heard the same things from our preacher at church, but from my own personal experience.

My first memory of a prayer that changed something in my life, occurred when I was around seven years old. I came home from playing in the woods with some type of infection. I was scared and crying, as parts of my body had begun to swell and throb, turning a purplish color. Mom quickly examined me, but was baffled when she found no snake bites, ticks, wounds or any explanation for the symptoms.

Calling an ambulance wasn't an option, as this was long-ago in rural Indiana, where the nearest hospital was a twenty-mile drive. Besides this, dad had the car and was away at work, so she explained that we would have to pray and ask God for His help.

I knew nothing about theology, but I believed in God. I also believed in my mom and her prayers... and desperately didn't want to go to the doctor or to the hospital. She laid me on the couch, put her hands on me and began to pray in her comforting voice. *"Lord Jesus, we ask you to take away this infection, heal Dale's body, make him well."* And then she looked me and added, *"but if you're not better in the morning, we'll have to take you to see the doctor."* That added warning made me especially aware of the need for God's help, and I remember also praying until I fell asleep.

To my amazement, when I awoke the following morning all the swelling and symptoms were gone! No one had to explain anything further to me, I knew what had happened. God answered our prayers! We never knew for sure what had made me ill, but I discovered years later that I had acquired an immunity to poison ivy/oak at some point. My speculation is that God may have healed me of a severe case of poison ivy, from which I emerged with an immunity that remains to this day.

I never forgot that experience, or grandma's prayer plaque on her wall... and when I grew up and had personal troubles of my own, I remembered how that praying to God can change things with life's many problems. More than a few times, I've applied His promise of Psalms 91:15, where the Lord says *"He shall call upon Me, and I will answer him; I will be with him in trouble; I will deliver him and honor him."*

God's intervention in my circumstances and difficulties has been many over the years. However, the greatest change He has brought about through my prayers, has been to me personally... starting when I responded to the message of the Gospel and became a follower of the Lord Jesus Christ. This is usually the first place where prayer's impact is felt, within the person who does the praying. It seems that the Lord begins answering our prayers "from the inside out," that is, working in us to bring about His will. In Ephesians 3:20, Paul said that the Lord *"is able to do exceedingly abundantly above all that we ask or think, according to the power that works in us."*

3

Prayer opens the channel of our heart to God's presence, who brings comfort, encouragement and strength... and who changes, shapes and molds us as we pray and yield our lives to Him. Ironically, He does much of this subtly as we presume to pray about other things. I can't tell you how many times I've knelt to pray, asking God to change situations, only to find that God changed "my" attitude toward those situations. Or instances when I prayed for God to vindicate me before my adversaries, only to find that He softened my heart toward them and gave me forgiveness instead.

But of course, prayer not only affects us internally, but as Jesus said in Mark 11:23-24, prayer combined with faith can also literally move mountains... or intervene with problems, or change situations that we can do nothing about. He said, *"whatever things you ask when you pray, believe that you receive them, and you will have them."*

Even when things seem impossible, nothing is beyond God's ability to change or completely reverse the most difficult situations. In Luke 1:37, Jesus said *"For with God nothing will be impossible."* God specializes in doing impossible, miraculous things, and is only limited by our ability to believe. Again, He said *"If you can believe, all things are possible to him who believes" (Mark 9:23).*

As long as you know your request fits into the pattern of God's will as shown in the Bible, never hesitate to be courageous in your faith. You can be assured that God will hear and answer such prayers. *"Now this is the confidence that we have in Him, that if we ask anything according to His will, He hears us. And if we know that He hears us, whatever we ask, we know that we have the petitions that we have asked of Him" (1 John 5:14-15).*

Jesus wants us to bring our every need, issue or crisis to Him in prayer, and to trust Him to work out His plan for our life. He doesn't want us to worry or fret, but to rest in Him to be our helper and provider. *"Don't worry about anything; instead, pray about everything. Tell God what you need, and thank him for all he has done"* *(Philippians 4:6 NLT).*

Finally, Andrew Murray, the famed 19th century minister who was known for his writings on prayer, wrote this unforgettable nugget about the benefit of praying to God: *"Time spent in prayer will yield more than that given to work. Prayer alone gives work its worth and its success. Prayer opens the way for God Himself to do His work in us and through us."*[1]

[1] *The ministry of intercession, a plea for more prayer, Andrew Murray, 1898*

2. What is Prayer?

For the Christian, the idea of prayer can be defined in a variety of ways. I generally describe prayer as *"an expression of our heart toward God, conversing with Him by words or thoughts."* E.M. Bounds, the famed 19th century author and clergyman, wrote simply that *"Prayer is the language of a man burdened with a sense of need."*[1] And perhaps one of the best and most quoted definitions, comes from Evangelist Billy Graham, who once said, *"Prayer is spiritual communication between man and God, a two-way relationship in which man should not only talk to God but also listen to Him. Prayer to God is like a child's conversation with his father."*[2]

Scripture shows that the prayers of early believers were directed toward either the Heavenly Father through

Jesus' name, or specifically to the Lord Jesus Christ *(Acts 7:59, Ephesians 5:20)*. But apart from understanding who to pray to, the most important thing would be to pray with belief and sincerity, expecting Him to reply in some fashion. Besides wanting to bring answers to our prayers, the Lord also desires to simply commune with us. He often does this by imparting a sense of His peace and encouragement, or perhaps by communicating His thoughts or words to our heart... what some call His "still small voice."

Prayer can be personalized in any variety of ways. It can be occasional or constant, long or short, spontaneous or formal. Prayer can also be secret or public, thankful or remorseful... or can consist of worship, thanksgiving, music or praise. Prayer can convey your requests, or simply unburden your heart... anytime, anywhere... standing, kneeling, lying, or even as you work or do other things. I've even found myself praying in my sleep, dreaming of prayers that I was expressing to God.

Prayer can also be modeled after the scores of examples recorded in scripture, such as the many Psalms that expressed David's prayers. His prayer of repentance in Psalm 51 is one of the most touching and remorseful prayers in the Bible, and provides a remarkable example of how we should pray for forgiveness when we have sinned. Even just a few verses of this heartrending appeal to God, moves me to tears nearly every time I read it. Two of the more notable verses read, *"Create in me a clean heart, O God. Renew a loyal spirit within me. Do not banish me from your presence, and don't take your Holy Spirit from me. Restore to me the joy of your salvation, and make me willing to obey you" (Psalms 51:10-12 NLT).*

Obviously, the greatest model for prayer, is the lesson Jesus gave to his disciples of how to pray in the 6th chapter of Matthew's gospel (which I share in greater detail elsewhere in this writing). The Lord's Prayer, as we commonly call it, has been a sacred prayer recited by believers for centuries, however Jesus intended it to also serve as a guideline or template for prayers in general.

Like many others in my day, I memorized the Lord's Prayer from the King James vernacular, which remains as the most frequently quoted source. But reading this familiar passage from a newer version, such as the New Living Translation, provides fresh meaning and value to the treasured words:

Jesus said, *"When you pray, don't babble on and on as people of other religions do. They think their prayers are answered merely by repeating their words again and again. Don't be like them, for your Father knows exactly what you need even before you ask him! Pray like this: Our Father in heaven, may your name be kept holy. May your Kingdom come soon. May your will be done on earth, as it is in heaven. Give us today the food we need, and forgive us our sins, as we have forgiven those who sin against us. And don't let us yield to temptation, but rescue us from the evil one"* (Matthew 6:7-13 NLT).

Finally, and most importantly, always remember that prayer is much more than just placing your order at a drive-up window. Prayer is the practice of relationship, an act of spiritual fellowship and intimacy with your Heavenly Father, the One who loves and cares about you more than anyone else in the world.

[1] *The Necessity of Prayer, E. M. Bounds, 1922*
[2] *What is prayer?, Billy Graham Evangelistic Association, 2004*

3. Does God Hear Me When I Pray?

If you are a follower of the Lord, Yes, He hears your prayers. *"For the eyes of the Lord are on the righteous, And His ears are open to their prayers; But the face of the Lord is against those who do evil" (1 Peter 3:12).*

If you are not a follower of the Lord, there is no assurance that God will respond to your prayers, as the scripture says, *"Now we know that God does not hear sinners; but if anyone is a worshiper of God and does His will, He hears him" (John 9:31).* David also knew this to be fact, and indicated that if he was aware of unforgiven sin in his heart, it would hinder his prayers from being answered. *"If I regard iniquity in my heart, The Lord will not hear" (Psalms 66:18).*

Of course, God is sovereign and can do things however He wants... and I've known many people who have prayed and talked to the Lord long before ever becoming His follower. Soldiers who cry out to God in foxholes, or persons who plea for help from the unknown God. He alone can see the content of hearts, and without doubt has responded at times to such sincere expressions, extending His mercy with a desire to bring such souls into a relationship with Him.

However, the first prayer you can be "assured" that He will hear and answer, is when you ask Him to forgive your sins and to come into your heart. The scripture says, *"For whoever calls on the name of the Lord shall be saved" (Romans 10:13).* And John writes, *"If we confess our sins, He is faithful and just to forgive us our sins and to cleanse us from all unrighteousness" (1 John 1:9).*

8

The person who is made right with God, and who begins following the Lord's will, seeking to please Him with their life, can approach the Lord with confidence that He will hear their prayers *(1 John 3:21-22)*. *"Let us therefore come boldly to the throne of grace, that we may obtain mercy and find grace to help in time of need" (Hebrews 4:16)*.

4. How Can I get Answers to Prayer?

One of history's most famous quotes regarding prayer, comes from Christ's sermon on the mount, where He said, *"Ask, and it will be given to you; seek, and you will find; knock, and it will be opened to you. For everyone who asks receives, and he who seeks finds, and to him who knocks it will be opened" (Matthew 7:7-8)*.

Jesus clearly promised that praying to God makes a difference, and that such persistence can eventually obtain results. But as He and his Apostles elaborate in scripture, answers to prayer involve other conditions and contingencies that must also be considered. **The following are five such principles toward obtaining answered prayers:**

(1) Become a follower of Christ – The first thing to understand is that answers to prayer are a benefit that Christ promises exclusively to His followers. In other words, to be eligible to get answered prayers, a person must become a follower of Jesus Christ. The Bible offers no assurance that God will listen to the prayers of anyone else, as this passage suggests: *"Now we know that God does not hear sinners; but if anyone is a worshiper of God and does His will, He hears him" (John 9:31)*.

9

Similar thoughts were echoed by Peter, who described God's openness toward the prayers of the righteous, in contrast to those who pursue a life of wickedness. *"For the eyes of the Lord are on the righteous, And His ears are open to their prayers; But the face of the Lord is against those who do evil" (1 Peter 3:12).*

Fortunately, it's not complicated to become a Christian. Jesus promises that He will turn no one away who calls upon Him for salvation. *"For whoever calls on the name of the Lord shall be saved" (Romans 10:13).* If you have never experienced the new birth that Jesus described in John 3:3, we provide a good outline at the back of this book that explains how to receive Christ's great gift of salvation and His forgiveness for sin *(John 3:16, Romans 3:23, 6:23, 5:8, 10:9-10).*

(2) Submit Your Life to God's Will – The Bible associates answers to prayer with the idea of being strongly committed in your faith relationship with God, devoted to pleasing Him, and submitting yourself to His will. *"Beloved, if our heart does not condemn us, we have confidence toward God. And whatever we ask we receive from Him, because we keep His commandments and do those things that are pleasing in His sight. And this is His commandment: that we should believe on the name of His Son Jesus Christ and love one another, as He gave us commandment" (1 John 3:21-23).*

The idea of submission to God's will, goes beyond the concept of a casual association. Jesus explained that a profession of Christ, without devotion to God's will and desires, is hollow and insufficient to take anyone to Heaven. He said, *"Not everyone who says to Me, 'Lord,*

Lord,' shall enter the kingdom of heaven, but he who does the will of My Father in heaven" (Matthew 7:21).

Those who seek to please the Lord will not only comply with His command to love one another, but will also attempt to put Him and His will at the forefront of their lives. When believers strive to submit themselves to His desires, and make it their priority to pursue the values of God's kingdom and righteousness, not only will they receive answers to prayer... but Jesus said they can expect a natural flow of blessing and provision "added" into their lives. *"But seek first the kingdom of God and His righteousness, and all these things shall be added to you" (Matthew 6:33). (See also Psalms 37:4-5)*

Jesus summed all this up another way. He said, *"If you abide in Me, and My words abide in you, you will ask what you desire, and it shall be done for you" (John 15:7).* His meaning was that if you continue in a right relationship with Christ, and allow His Word and principles to become the core of your whole being, you'll receive what you ask of the Lord... because His Will and Word, will have become the basis for your entire life and desires. *George Mueller once said, "Be assured, if you walk with Him and look to Him, and expect help from Him, He will never fail you."*[1]

(3) Ask in His Will – It should be no surprise, that if our lives must be conformed to God's will, so must be the things that we ask Him for. The Lord does not obligate Himself to hear any prayer that is based on evil, impure motives, or contrary to His desires. *"You ask and do not receive, because you ask amiss, that you may spend it on your pleasures" (James 4:3).* But if we know that our requests are in compliance with His will, we can have assurance that He will honor our requests. *"Now this is* *the confidence that we have in Him, that if we ask anything according to His will, He hears us. And if we know that He hears us, whatever we ask, we know that we have the petitions that we have asked of Him" (1 John 5:14-15).*

People often waste their time and energy, pleading for God to bless something, or grant a request that He opposes or has no interest in. This has often caused needless frustration and disillusionment, as persons can't figure out why their prayers go unanswered. God is not the genie of a magic lamp, whose purpose is to comply with your whims and wishes. Rather, He is God Almighty, your Creator, the King of Kings... and it's your purpose to serve Him, and honor His wishes... which are consistently pure, holy, and always in the best interest of His beloved children.

The better idea is to find out what God desires for you... and it won't be hard to persuade Him to answer those kinds of prayer requests. If you *"seek first the kingdom of God and His righteousness,"* it will involve spiritual devotion, prayer, study of God's word, and pursuing a Godly lifestyle, that will help bring clarity to His will, and guidance for your life.

Praying the scriptures is one of the best ways to keep the focus of our prayers in God's will. Seek out the promises in God's Word that pertain to your needs, and plead your case to the Lord on the basis of His promises. Quote them back to the Lord in your prayers, expressing thanks and assurance for what He has promised to do. Obviously, God is not forgetful of what He has said or promised, but is especially pleased when we know His Word, and are willing to stake our trust and confidence in what He has said. There is little else that thrills God more, than to be taken at His Word.

(4) Ask in Faith – One of the most important things to learn about God, is to understand the enormous value He places on faith. Righteousness was imputed to Abraham because He believed God *(Romans 4:3)*, and is the very same basis for our redemption and salvation through our Lord Jesus Christ *(Ephesians 2:8-9)*. Faith is essentially believing in the reality of someone or some thing, that you can't see or perceive with natural senses *(Hebrews 11:1)* ... and there is nothing else that pleases God more, than for you to believe in His reality, or to trust the veracity of His Word, without any visible or tangible evidence. Persistent, passionate prayers of faith please God, in that they express confidence that He will hear us, help us, and respond to our pleas. *"But without faith it is impossible to please Him, for he who comes to God must believe that He is, and that He is a rewarder of those who diligently seek Him" (Hebrews 11:6).*

To get results from your prayers, you must pray in faith... not only believing that God hears you, but by "taking possession" of His promise by faith. *"Therefore I say to you, whatever things you ask when you pray, believe that you receive them, and you will have them" (Mark 11:24).*

Such faith is not a matter of "pretending" something is real, but is a confidence derived from His Word... that, though yet unseen, God has heard and answered our prayer. As John said, *"we know that we have the petitions that we have asked of Him" (1 John 5:15).*

Such confidence converts our pleading prayers into prayers of thanksgiving and praise... expressing faith for what God already considers done and accomplished, though not yet tangible or seen in our present state.

How Faith Works

The Bible defines faith in an interesting way, explaining that *"faith is the substance of things hoped for, the evidence of things not seen," (Hebrews 11:1).* On one hand, faith has tangible characteristics of "substance" and "reality," yet on the other hand is "unseen" and "intangible" to our natural senses. This sounds quite mysterious and contradictory, until we look further to the 3rd verse, and can see what the writer is trying to convey. Essentially, faith has the same characteristics as the Word of God... that powerful invisible force that created the entire universe and all visible things. *"By faith we understand that the worlds were framed by the word of God, so that the things which are seen were not made of things which are visible" (Hebrews 11:3).* Likewise, faith also expresses confidence in realities not yet seen, because it is the same very nature of God and His Word, who *"calls those things that be not, as though they were" (Romans 4:17 KJV).*

Consequently, faith, which *"comes by hearing, and hearing by the word of God" (Romans 10:17),* is a combination of our agreement with God's Word... and shares the same characteristics and awesome potential. In other words, faith is as powerful as God's Word, because that's really what it is... it's the Word of God deployed by means of our agreement through prayer and faith. Faith expresses the same thing that the Word of God expresses... another reason why quoting from God's Word and promises in our prayers can be important.

14

The declaration of our words is important to our faith relationship to God's Word. That is, our heart and words both need to come into agreement with what God's Word says. This is the pattern of "believing" and "confessing" that Paul described as it pertains to our faith for salvation. He said, *"If you confess with your mouth that Jesus is Lord and believe in your heart that God raised him from the dead, you will be saved. For it is by believing in your heart that you are made right with God, and it is by confessing with your mouth that you are saved"* (Romans 10:9-10 NLT).

"Confess" comes from the Greek, *"Homologeo"* (ὁμολογέω) which essentially means to "agree with" or "say the same words." What this suggests, is that if your heart believes the Gospel message that Jesus is Lord, then the words of your mouth should agree with that too.

I can speak from my own experience of having led hundreds of persons into a relationship with Christ, that until a new believer declares that "Jesus is their Lord," something is not yet complete. In addition to bringing glory to God, this is at least in-part why Jesus required believers to confess and acknowledge Him before others *(Matthew 10:32-33)*.

So why should this pattern be any different with other applications of faith in God's promises? Personally, when I have needs, I apply this same template of faith. I come before the Lord in prayer, stating my case based upon His Word.

For instance, if I'm ill and need His help and healing, besides calling the elders of the church to pray and anoint me with oil *(James 5:1-15)*, I will pray something like this:

"Dear Lord, I come to you in Jesus name, obeying what you told me to do in Matthew 7:7. You said, 'Ask, and it will be given to me, seek, and I will find; knock, and it will be opened to me.' I'm asking and believing for you to make me well, just as your Word tells me not to forget your benefits, that you forgive all my iniquities, and heal all my diseases (Psalms 103:2-3)."

"Lord, not once did you ever turn anyone away for healing during your earthly ministry, nor do I believe that you will turn me away. You promised that if I ask anything according to your will, you hear me... and that I can be assured of the answer that I've asked of you (1 John 5:14-15). So, Lord Jesus, I believe that you bore my sins and sickness on the cross, and I hold fast to your Word that says... 'But He was wounded for our transgressions, He was bruised for our iniquities; The chastisement for our peace was upon Him, And by His stripes we are healed' (Isaiah 53:5)."

Not only is this my prayer, but also my declaration of faith in His promises, believing that He has heard my prayer and is bringing about the answer. During my continuing prayers, I'll keep thanking God and declaring my confidence in His promises in a similar fashion. And if my heart grows weary or discouraged, perhaps from the pain or symptoms reminding me that my body is still sick, I'll drop to my knees to pray, and keep expressing thanksgiving and my faith in His promises. I will pray, worship and quote His promises continually until I sense His peace and confidence return to my heart.

If someone asks how I'm doing, I'll not speak a falsehood by claiming that my symptoms are gone if they are still present... but I will instead express my faith in God's

Word. *"Well, brother, regardless how I feel, I've embraced the Lord's promise for my healing, and that's the truth that I'm standing on. I believe His Word that says He forgives all MY iniquities, and heals all MY diseases (Psalms 103:2-3)."*

(5) Keep Believing and Remain Persistent and Patient – When I first became a believer and started learning about prayer and faith, I sometimes imagined prayers as though they were explosions of spiritual energy. I often thought that if persons could just pray powerfully enough at a given time or place, it would get God's attention, insomuch he'd bring the answer or miracle on the spot.

However, as I began growing in God's Word, learning to pray and receiving answers to my prayers... I could see that prayer and faith works somewhat different than I originally thought. While there are indeed fervent, anointed prayers that prove especially effective at given moments *(James 5:16)*, most of our success in prayer appears to comes from prolonged durations of faith and persistence. This means to keep praying and believing, day after day... to continue standing on God's promises, thanking Him for the answer, despite the absence of any encouraging signs... or even in the face of adversity or discouragement.

What I learned was that faith is not measured by its amplitude alone, but together with its frequency. In other words, the effectiveness of prayer is not usually the result of an explosive burst of faith, but is from the combined day-to-day persistence and consistency to pray and believe. If you are committed to the "long haul" of prayer, you'll eventually get to your destination... just don't give up. As someone once said, *"whenever you're determined to pray no matter how long it takes to get an answer, it generally doesn't take long."*

One of the greatest teachings about persistent prayer, comes from the Lord's parable of the widow and unjust judge. *"Then He spoke a parable to them, that men always ought to pray and not lose heart, saying: There was in a certain city a judge who did not fear God nor regard man. Now there was a widow in that city; and she came to him, saying, Get justice for me from my adversary. And he would not for a while; but afterward he said within himself, Though I do not fear God nor regard man, yet because this widow troubles me I will avenge her, lest by her continual coming she weary me. Then the Lord said, Hear what the unjust judge said. And shall God not avenge His own elect who cry out day and night to Him, though He bears long with them? I tell you that He will avenge them speedily. Nevertheless, when the Son of Man comes, will He really find faith on the earth?" (Luke 18:1-8).*

The great lesson of this parable is seen in the Heavenly Father's contrast with the unjust judge. Our God, of course, is not unjust in any way, but is in fact the "righteous" judge of the entire universe... who's desire is not to resist your petitions, or drag his feet from bringing His intervention. As Jesus explained, if even an earthly magistrate will eventually tire and acquiesce to such persistence, how much more eagerly will our Lord respond to your enduring perseverance and faith?

The need for patience is something seldom appreciated in today's fast-food, instant download society. However, this and similar passages remind us that it is a necessary part of the faith process... and that our determination will eventually be rewarded. God is truly *"a rewarder of those who diligently seek Him."*

Be encouraged, as God is a loving and merciful God, who desires to help you. So, let's do as the scripture says, *"Let us therefore come boldly to the throne of grace, that we may obtain mercy and find grace to help in time of need"* *(Hebrews 4:16).*

[1] *George Müller of Bristol, Arthur Tappan Pierson, 1899*

5. What Kind of Things Can I Pray For?

Basically, you can take any issues of concern to God in prayer. He cares about all aspects of your life... and wants to bring His blessing, guidance, comfort and provision in every way *(Matthew 6:25-34).* The salvation of your soul, and matters pertaining to your spiritual life, are of great importance to Him, but He also cares about your physical health, your finances, your career, marriage, family and so forth. The Apostle Paul wrote, *"Don't worry about anything; instead, pray about everything. Tell God what you need, and thank him for all he has done"* *(Philippians 4:6 NLT).*

The Lord desires to bring His followers a life of purpose and meaning, filled with the righteousness, peace and joy of the Holy Spirit *(Romans 14:17).* And He appeals to those weighed down with problems and burdens, to come to Him for His strength. He said, *"Come to me, all you who are weary and burdened, and I will give you rest"* *(Matthew 11:28).* Peter put it this way, *"Give all your worries and cares to God, for he cares about you" (1 Peter 5:7 NLT).*

The Bible says that God will hear and answer any of His children's prayer requests that conform to His will and desires. In other words, what we ask must be what God wants... as there's no assurance God will answer prayers that are out of harmony with His will. *"Now this is the confidence that we have in Him, that if we ask anything according to His will, He hears us. And if we know that He hears us, whatever we ask, we know that we have the petitions that we have asked of Him" (1 John 5:14-15).*

The psalmist described this in another way... to make it your objective to find joy in serving and pleasing the Lord, and He will fulfill your heart's desires. *"Delight yourself also in the Lord, And He shall give you the desires of your heart. Commit your way to the Lord, Trust also in Him, And He shall bring it to pass" (Psalms 37:4-5).* In this same regard, Andrew Murray wrote, *"We may be sure that, as we delight in what God delights in, such prayer is inspired by God and will have its answer."*[1]

Keep in mind, God always reserves the right to answer prayers as He sees fit. Out of His wisdom, love and mercy, He may deny some prayer requests... or else answer some prayers in a way that better fits into His plan and will for one's life. But when we commit ourselves to Him and His Ways, we can trust that He will always be working in the background, to bring about His good plan and purpose. *"And we know that all things work together for good to those who love God, to those who are the called according to His purpose" (Romans 8:28).*

Prayer, of course, is not only intended to bring your personal matters to the Lord's attention, but also to intercede for the needs and problems of others. *"I urge you, first of all, to pray for all people. Ask God to help them; intercede on their behalf, and give thanks for them" (1 Timothy 2:1).*

Search through the scriptures, as they have much more to say about the things we can or should pray for.

6. Can I Receive Healing Through Prayer?

Yes, God will honor faith-filled prayer, combined with other scriptural regimen, to bring about healing. This is due to the fact that healing is a part of Christ's great atonement that He provided through His sufferings and sacrificial death on the cross.

Man's sin and fall in the Garden brought separation from God's fellowship, resulting in the curse of sickness and death *(Genesis 3:17-19)*. However, the Heavenly Father sent Jesus to endure the sufferings and the brutal execution on the cross, as our substitute for that curse, so that all those who believe in Him could have a "bridge" back into the fellowship and benefits of God. *"For He made Him who knew no sin to be sin for us, that we might become the righteousness of God in Him" (2 Corinthians 5:21).*

Jesus not only purchased the salvation of our soul, but His sufferings also secured your physical healing. Years before Christ came to the earth, the prophet Isaiah described the future sufferings of the coming Savior and their purpose. He wrote, *"Surely He has borne our griefs and carried our*

21

sorrows; yet we esteemed Him stricken, smitten by God, and afflicted. But He was wounded for our transgressions, He was bruised for our iniquities; the chastisement for our peace was upon Him, and by His stripes we are healed" (Isaiah 53:4-5).

The stripes mentioned by Isaiah were the awful lashings upon Jesus' back by the Roman whips. Thirty-nine stripes were the traditional punishment for a condemned prisoner. According to the scripture, these stripes upon Christ were in behalf of our spiritual and physical healing, *"who Himself bore our sins in His own body on the tree, that we, having died to sins, might live for righteousness-- by whose stripes you were healed"* (1 Peter 2:24).

Salvation and healing are tied closely together throughout the scriptures, often mentioned in the same breath, such as in this psalm. *"Bless the Lord, O my soul, And forget not all His benefits: Who forgives all your iniquities, Who heals all your diseases"* (Psalms 103:2-3). As a matter of fact, the word "salvation" so frequently used in the New Testament, comes from the Greek, *SOTERIA (σωτηρία)*, which means "wholeness and healing, both in the physical and spiritual."

Ironically, Jesus explained that the miracles of healing that He performed during His ministry, were to demonstrate His authority to also forgive sins, which he did for a paralyzed man in Capernaum. When some of the Jewish leaders saw and heard Jesus' claim, they were outraged by such blasphemy... as they knew that only God alone had the authority to forgive sins and heal sicknesses. How shocked they must have been, when Jesus then healed the paralytic, exposing His true divine identity. He said, *"For which is easier, to say, 'Your sins are forgiven you,' or to say, 'Arise and walk'? But that you may know that the Son of Man has power on earth to forgive sins--then He said to the paralytic, Arise, take up your bed, and go to your house" (Matthew 9:5-6).*

7. Does it Help to Have Others Pray with Me?

Yes, absolutely! The Bible indicates that the effectiveness of prayer is amplified when multiple believers combine and unify their faith. Even as few as two who come into agreement in prayer, can have a powerful effect. *"I also tell you this: If two of you agree here on earth concerning anything you ask, my Father in heaven will do it for you. For where two or three gather together as my followers, I am there among them" (Matthew 18:19-20 NLT).*

Time and again, I've witnessed the amazing results of believers praying together in agreement for various needs... and have always conveyed the importance of this principle to the many congregations we've ministered to. In my view, Jesus' promise to bring His presence to wherever two or more are gathered in His name, and to answer their prayers of faith and agreement, is one of the most astounding promises in the Bible. This something that Christians need to appreciate and implement every time they meet.

An example of this can be seen in scripture, when the church body prayed together for Peter, who had been arrested and jailed by King Herod. *"...while Peter was in prison, the church prayed very earnestly for him" (Acts 12:5 NLT).* And as they prayed, an angel appeared to Peter and miraculously led him out of the prison, but when he soon came knocking at their door, most could not believe it was him! Though a servant girl recognized it was Peter, many scoffed and even assumed it had to be his deceased spirit, until they finally opened the door and realized it was really him! *(Acts 12:5-15)*. I have chuckled at this many times... to think how they were praying for a miracle of Peter's deliverance, and then couldn't believe it when he showed up at the door. Hopefully, if any others of us pray similarly for such miracles, it won't come as a surprise when it happens!

This reminds me of a series of nightly church meetings we held in Indiana years ago, in which we would conclude each service in prayer for various needs or burdens. As different ones shared their needs, one woman made the same request each night... for her husband to come to church and get saved. As I recall, she explained that he was a drunk who opposed her relationship with God, and even opposed her going to church. Each night we prayed in agreement for various needs, including this man.

Finally, during the closing meeting on Sunday night, we ended the service with prayer at the altar... and while we were again praying for the woman's husband, I saw a stranger stumble in the back door of the church and begin staggering down the center aisle. When he reached the front where we were gathered, the woman was shocked... it was her husband, who that night knelt and surrendered his heart to Christ! And most amazing thing of all, he had no idea how he got to the church, nor did he know this was the church his wife attended!

The combined prayers of other believers are also especially effective when praying for healing. The bible says that when you are ill, you should ask elders (plural) of the church to come pray over you, promising that their prayers of faith will make them well. *"Is anyone among you sick? Let him call for the elders of the church, and let them pray over him, anointing him with oil in the name of the Lord. And the prayer of faith will save the sick, and the Lord will raise him up. And if he has committed sins, he will be forgiven" (James 5:14-15).*

When we pray for the sick, we usually follow this pattern described above by James. A church elder or elders anoints the sick persons with oil (a symbol of the Holy Spirit), and prays the prayer of faith. But we may also combine this with Christ's promise of Matthew 18:19-20, by inviting our other fellow believers to unify their faith with ours, as we all pray and believe together for the Lord to perform the healing.

If your church has prayer gatherings or corporate prayer meetings (which I think all churches should have), you should participate. If it doesn't, offer to help your church start one. If there's anything that a church should be about, it should be prayer. Quoting from Isaiah 56:7, Jesus said, *"It is written, 'My house shall be called a house of prayer'" (Matthew 21:13).*

When in need of prayer, such meetings are a good place to come request the combined prayers from your fellow believers. It's also a tremendous opportunity for you to join with combined prayer for others, as well as for the pastor and the church. Basically, all believers need prayer... and we all are charged with the responsibility of praying for each other. *"Stay alert and be persistent in your prayers for all believers everywhere" (Ephesians 6:18 NLT).*

Sadly, church prayer meetings have become so poorly attended in recent years, many congregations have simply given up trying to maintain them. This really is nothing new, since as far back as the 19th century, Charles Finney said, *"Prayer meetings are the most difficult meetings to sustain because they are the most spiritual meetings of the church."*

However, nothing will help and strengthen the ministry of the church or the pastor more than prayer. In fact, I saw a clever phrase along this theme some time ago: *"If your church thinks it needs a better preacher, pray for the one you've got!"* How true this is! And not only will a praying church enjoy the fruit of God's favor... it cannot hope to achieve any meaningful successes without it. Jesus wasn't kidding when He said, *"without Me you can do nothing"* *(John 15:5).*

People rarely understand the great need to pray for their church and leaders, who deal with enormous spiritual challenges. Besides just doing their best to survive the modern trends of declining attendance, so they can minister to people who generally have overwhelming problems, pastors also frequently struggle with their own personal difficulties. Church members may not realize that clergymen often suffer some of the highest occurrences of stress related illnesses. And since they often find the challenges of ministry so great, it's been reported that hundreds of pastors quit the ministry each month. And in case you've not noticed, in recent years the body of Christ in America, has become an increased target of persecution and hostility, spewed freely by anti-Christian groups, the news media, as well as our own government.

Never have the forces of darkness been more intensely focused on the church of Jesus Christ. But Praise God, He has given us the spiritual weaponry of prayer to face and overcome these assaults! Through such prayer, the Gospel of Christ can continue to move forward and flow freely with the desired effect of bringing souls into the Kingdom of God. *"For the weapons of our warfare are not carnal but mighty in God for pulling down strongholds" (2 Corinthians 10:4).*

8. Is Prayer Meant Only to "Ask" God for Things?

No. Obviously, God cares about your needs and the things that concern you, and wants you to ask for His help... but prayer goes far beyond this. To begin with, prayer is meant to be a spiritual "conversation" between you and God. It's intended as two-way channel in which we not only talk to God, but can also listen to Him. When you pray, take time also to be still and wait upon the Lord and allow Him to speak your heart.

Prayer is also an act of spiritual intimacy and fellowship that draws you closer to the Lord's presence. In his famed devotional, Oswald Chambers wrote, *"It is a joy to Jesus when a person takes time to walk more intimately with Him. The bearing of fruit is always shown in Scripture to be a visible result of an intimate relationship with Jesus Christ."*[1]

The Free Dictionary describes prayer as *"a spiritual communion with God or an object of worship, as in supplication, thanksgiving, adoration, or confession."* A good example of this can be seen when Paul and Silas prayed and also sang hymns of worship and devotion to

God from their prison cell. *"Around midnight Paul and Silas were praying and singing hymns to God, and the other prisoners were listening" (Acts 16:25 NLT).*

The book of Psalms shows how David (who authored many of the psalms) worshiped and sang as he prayed to the Lord. *"But each day the Lord pours his unfailing love upon me, and through each night I sing his songs, praying to God who gives me life" (Psalms 42:8 NLT).* The whole book, in fact, is a collection of prayers, poems, and hymns that were intended to facilitate worship and adoration to God. Many of the Psalms were used as a hymnal in the ancient Jewish worship services, and the title, "psalms," comes from the idea of singing along with musical instruments.

Giving of thanks is another component of worship that's usually incorporated into prayer. Paul told Timothy, *"I urge you, first of all, to pray for all people. Ask God to help them; intercede on their behalf, and give thanks for them" (1 Timothy 2:1 NLT).*

Consequently, prayer can incorporate many components. Worship, singing, music, conversing with God, giving Him thanks... can be practiced individually, but can also merge into simultaneous expressions of prayer or spiritual fellowship with God.

The bottom line is that prayer brings you closer to God's presence, who is then able to deepen your spiritual roots and strength. *"Draw near to God and He will draw near to you" (James 4:8). "The Lord is near to all who call upon Him, To all who call upon Him in truth" (Psalms 145:18).*

[1] *Intimate with Jesus, My Utmost for His Highest, Oswald Chambers, 1935*

9. How Can I Pray in God's Will?

The Bible tells us that if we ask anything according to God's will, He will hear and answer such prayers. *"Now this is the confidence that we have in Him, that if we ask anything according to His will, He hears us. And if we know that He hears us, whatever we ask, we know that we have the petitions that we have asked of Him" (1 John 5:14-15).* But how can we know that our prayer requests are in God's will?

First, God's Word is an expression of His will, so when you pray in accordance to the things He has promised or declared in the Bible, you can be assured that you're praying in His will. The late Christian painter, Thomas Kinkade, once wrote, *"The power of prayer is like turning on a light as it illuminates God's purpose for our lives. There is no greater connection to knowing His will other than the Word."*[1]

On the other hand, there are other specific or personal matters that are not directly addressed in scripture. For instance, while we know that it's the Lord will to meet your needs and provide you a job, what if you find yourself with a variety of career options? How can you tell which one is the Lord's will for your life? Which career path do you pray for?

In this or similar cases, you can pray and trust Him to lead and guide you toward decisions that most closely identify with God's character or desires (as shown in the Bible). Obviously, it will not be the Lord's will to follow a path that will lead you away from Him, or require for you to be dishonest, immoral or sinful. But we can't always forecast such pitfalls for every option that comes before us. This is why we must trust in His unseen guidance, even when it doesn't make sense to us. *"Trust in the Lord with all your heart, And lean not on your own understanding; In all your ways acknowledge Him, And He shall direct your paths" (Proverbs 3:5-6).*

It would be an easy thing to make all decisions if God would just speak to us in an audible voice and tell us His will, but that doesn't always happen. To seek out His will, open the Word of God and pray, ask Him to lead and guide you "according to His will." Sometimes His guidance will come as an "inclination" or perhaps a "still small voice." At other times, we may need to take steps forward by faith, trusting God to give us the right choice when the time comes. *"Teach me to do your will, for you are my God. May your gracious Spirit lead me forward on a firm footing" (Psalms 143:10 NLT).*

There are also moments when we are simply at a loss of what to pray, and yet the Holy Spirit can intervene and help us, by interceding through us according to the will of God. *"And the Holy Spirit helps us in our weakness. For example, we don't know what God wants us to pray for. But the Holy Spirit prays for us with groanings that cannot be expressed in words. And the Father who knows all hearts knows what the Spirit is saying, for the Spirit pleads for us believers in harmony with God's own will" (Romans 8:26-27 NLT).*

The most important thing is to yield your will to God's, to be willing to follow His will and path regardless of what or where that takes you. That may sometimes be challenging, but be assured that God's plan always works out better than your own. Even Jesus, who knew His purpose and the will of the Heavenly Father, wrestled with His flesh that was hesitant to follow that path of suffering and death. But had He not yielded His will to His Father's, the miracle of His resurrection would have never happened. On the night before His trial and crucifixion, Jesus prayed in the garden, *"O My Father, if it is possible, let this cup pass from Me; nevertheless, not as I will, but as You will" (Matthew 26:39).*

The struggle to submit our will to God's will is always the great challenge to our prayers. In fact, this is one of the most frequent reasons why some prayers go unanswered, in that persons often seek their own self-willed wants, lusts and desires, rather than God's. As James wrote, *"You ask and do not receive, because you ask amiss, that you may spend it on your pleasures" (James 4:3).*

Despite anyone's intensity or devotion to prayer, God's will can never be manipulated to bless anything that He considers to be unacceptable. The object of prayer is not merely what you want, but what "God" wants for you. Prayer is not calling on the Genie of a magic lamp, nor is it making a wish upon a star. Prayer is coming into harmony with the will of your Heavenly Father, and asking Him to fulfill His desires for your life.

[1] *Keep Me and Keep All, Robert W. Smith, 2011*

10. Can God Answer an Unbeliever's Prayers?

Prayer is intended as a privilege for Christians, those who believe and follow the Lord Jesus Christ in faith with their lives. If you're not a believer, there is no assurance that God will respond to your prayers. *"We know that God doesn't listen to sinners, but he is ready to hear those who*

worship him and do his will" *(John 9:31 NLT)*. Peter also
confirmed these same sentiments, quoting from Psalm
34:15, he said, *"The eyes of the Lord watch over those who
do right, and his ears are open to their prayers. But the
Lord turns his face against those who do evil"* *(1 Peter 3:12
NLT)*.

However, the great news is that you can become a believer
today and start living for God at this moment! This is the
first prayer you can be assured that He will answer, when
you ask Him to forgive your sins and to come into your
heart. The scripture says, *"for whoever calls on the name
of the Lord shall be saved"* *(Romans 10:13)*. And John
writes, *"If we confess our sins, He is faithful and just to
forgive us our sins and to cleanse us from all
unrighteousness"* *(1 John 1:9)*.

When a person is made right with God, and begins
following the Lord's will, seeking to please Him with their
life, they can approach the Lord with confidence that He
will hear their prayers. *"Beloved, if our heart does not
condemn us, we have confidence toward God. And
whatever we ask we receive from Him, because we keep His
commandments and do those things that are pleasing in
His sight"* *(1 John 3:21-22)*.

"Need" has often been the reason that many people have
come to the Lord to begin with. I've known of many who
became believers as they prayed and called on the Lord for
His help during their problems and troubles. In fact, I was
one such person.

When my life fell apart as a young man, I went to the Lord
in desperation, seeking His help. At first, I wasn't aware
that my greater need was actually to repent and be

forgiven of my sins. But along the way of my tearful pleas and prayers for other matters and problems, I also ended up asking Jesus to forgive my sins and to come into my heart. I think it works that way for a lot of people. They may initially come seeking the Lord's help for some other problem, but end up finding Jesus, the answer for all their problems.

This is often a reason why God may allow troubles or problems to come along, so that we will reach out to Him for His help. Consequently, one's difficulty may actually be a blessing in disguise, an opportunity to connect with God. Not only to seek His mercy and help for their need, but to discover His love and forgiveness as Lord and Savior. *"Seek the Lord while He may be found, Call upon Him while He is near. Let the wicked forsake his way, And the unrighteous man his thoughts; Let him return to the Lord, And He will have mercy on him; And to our God, For He will abundantly pardon"* (Isaiah 55:6-7).

Turn your life over to Christ. Serve Him, live for Him, and believe His Word. And you'll find that He will begin answering your prayers... and leading and guiding you in all kinds of amazing ways.

11. Will God Answer Prayers for Imperfect Believers?

The good news for you is... there are NO perfect Christians. Even the Apostle Paul, who wrote half the New Testament, and certainly received many answers to prayers, said that he struggled with sin and imperfection in his mortal flesh *(Romans 7:14-25)*.

Thus, because of the sin nature all humans are born with, it is not possible for any person to live a perfectly flawless life *(Romans 3:23)*. However, this is why Jesus came into the world, so that He could bridge this gap between sinful man and the Holy righteous God in Heaven. Jesus gave His life on the cross to pay for the penalty of man's sin (in God's law, sin demands death *Romans 6:23)*. And for every person who believes in Jesus and His atoning work on the cross... He brings forgiveness of their sins, along with the indwelling of His Spirit, whose nature is to obey and please the Lord.

What this means is, even though a Christian may be flawed, their faith in Christ procures His grace to forgive sins and impute righteousness in their heart... so they can continue to have access to God through their prayers. *"...people are counted as righteous, not because of their work, but because of their faith in God who forgives sinners" (Romans 4:4-5 NLT)*.

As a believer continues to follow Jesus daily, the instincts of Christ's nature will grow stronger and more influential in his lifestyle. This lifestyle "fruit" is the evidence that proves whether a person really has a faith relationship with Christ. If he does, he will continue to confess and turn away from sin *(1 John 1:9),* and will seek to yield his life to Christ's Spirit which manifests the nature of God's love... along with a desire to obey and please the Lord. *"If we love our Christian brothers and sisters, it proves that we have passed from death to life..." (1 John 3:14 NLT). (See also Ephesians 5:9, Galatians 5:22)*

So, though none of us are perfect, the Bible says that by faith believers can pray and come before the Lord's "throne of grace" to obtain His "mercy" in times of need.

"Grace" and "mercy" are not things that can be earned, but are expressions of unmerited favor, love, and forgiveness that God extends to those who believe. For this reason, we can come boldly before God's presence in faith, with assurance that he will hear our prayer. *"Let us therefore come boldly to the throne of grace, that we may obtain mercy and find grace to help in time of need" (Hebrews 4:16).*

12. Is it Possible to Pray for a Miracle?

Certainly. God is capable of performing such supernatural things in response to our prayers. The scripture even describes a specific gift of miracles, given by the Holy Spirit to the body of Christ *(1 Corinthians 12:10).*

However, what is a miracle? In the terminology of scripture, there are several words translated as miracle, which convey the general idea of supernatural signs, astonishing wonders that defy natural explanation, or dynamic works that demonstrate God's power, etc. Of the miracles described in the New Testament, most occurred instantaneously, right before their very eyes. Jesus, for instance, performed numerous miracles, such as of healings, expelling demons, raising persons from the dead. He even walked on the water, calmed a storm, and performed astonishing acts of provision such as feeding of the 5,000.

But even though an answer to prayer may not occur instantly, or seem as spectacular, it may be no less miraculous in its impact or value. In other words, what we interpret as a miracle, or a supernatural intervention by

God, can be a very subjective thing... sometimes only perceived as such, by the one for whom it occurs.

For example, I've received numerous answers to prayers in my lifetime, many of which seemed miraculous to me. The Lord intervened with problems that were impossible for me to overcome, or things I could not accomplish on my own. But for those who didn't witness these events, that often unfolded over a duration of time, they may not have recognized their miraculous impact upon me. Sometimes such common miracles are even overlooked by those who benefit from them.

Such was the case with a fellow I prayed for in an emergency room, decades ago. It began with an alarming late-night phone call, during the early months of my first pastorate. It was from Paula, a hospital emergency room nurse who attended our church. She regularly prayed for persons brought to the ER, and asked if I could come and join her in prayer for a young man who had been brought in from a horrible wreck, not expected to live.

I was glad to come pray, but wasn't really prepared to see his shocking condition. There in the bed laid the mangled body of an unconscious young male, hooked up with tubes and wires to every conceivable life-support contraption. The police said that while parking and exiting his car along a highway, Tom, a 20-year-old from the local community, stepped directly into the path of a semi-truck which hit and ran over him with its wheels. I overheard them say that none of the emergency responders had ever seen a victim injured this severely without dying.

Tom's body had been literally crushed and contorted. All his limbs and major bones were broken, and the internal damage to his organs was massive and devastating. After trying desperately to save his life, the doctors concluded that his injuries were beyond repair. There was nothing more they could do, and believed that his death was imminent.

When I arrived, and joined with Paula to pray for Tom, his terminal condition was a forgone conclusion, but despite the grim odds, we prayed for a miracle. I knew nothing about him, but from what I gathered he had apparently been under the influence of either alcohol or drugs, and I assumed that he did not know Christ. Without God's intervention, his premature death would not be the only tragedy, but to face eternity apart from Christ's forgiveness and salvation would be horrendous.

This was what motivated me most to pray and ask God for the impossible... for the soul of this young man. Not only is God a miracle maker *(Matthew 19:26)*, but I also know how much He loves mankind, and doesn't want anyone to be lost, *"not willing that any should perish but that all should come to repentance"* *(2 Peter 3:9)*. My plea to the Lord that night, was to give Tom another chance, that he might hear the Gospel, turn to Christ and be saved.

The following day I received a call from Paula, who told me that Tom had survived the night. The doctors were surprised, but still gave no hope of survival, as his injuries were too severe. But returning to the hospital, we prayed for him again, and to our joy he survived another night, and then another... which was beginning to cause the doctors to take notice. He remained in a coma, and they still maintained that his condition was hopeless, but now they were at least willing to keep looking for ways they might save him.

By this time, we had other folks praying for Tom in our church, and day after day his survival kept surprising the hospital staff. The doctors could not understand why he was still alive, but were pleased when his body began responding to their efforts. After the first week or so, they upgraded their outlook, giving him a slim chance of survival, which continued to improve slightly each day. Every time we came to pray, we would hear of more modest improvements... and after a couple weeks, he regained consciousness, and eventually began to speak.

Over the weeks, I made it a frequent routine to go visit and pray for Tom, whom the doctors now conceded that with extensive surgeries and treatment, would probably survive. But when they cautioned that he could never possibly walk again or live a normal life, I just smiled, knowing how far God had already brought him, and I didn't believe the Lord had any reason to stop answering our prayers now.

I had many chats with Tom about Jesus and His promise of salvation, and spoke with him about the numerous prayers that God had honored to help his survive. But to my amazement, Tom, who had no previous spiritual background, found it hard to accept God's miraculous intervention. He continued to think that his improvement was more to the credit of doctors and the hospital, which of course, God used in this process. But he never really understood that they had initially abandoned all hope and left him to die, and it was only an act of God's intervention that saved his life.

After many months I was reassigned to pastor a different congregation in a distant state, but before relocating, I went to visit Tom for a last time. I wasn't surprised to hear that he was now in physical therapy, showing signs that he might regain the ability to walk again. Indeed, while not instantaneous, God had answered scores of prayers, and performed a remarkable miracle in Tom's life. And I am hopeful that he eventually came to recognize that, appreciating the daily miracle of life that God restored to him.

In my view, this was nothing less than a miracle... a kind that happens a lot in response to prayers. But because such things may occur over a progression of time, people sometimes fail to see the big picture of God's involvement. The fact is, God answers prayer and performs miracles every day... and if only through small day-to-day increments, the eventual result is no less miraculous than if it occurred immediately. God also answers daily prayer for so many subtle or unnoticed things behind the scenes, to guide us, protect us, and to bring about His plan for our life. How thankful we should always be, for the unseen things God is doing in our behalf.

Probably the greatest miracle of all is the conversion of a soul... when a person's life is transformed by Christ, and they assume a brand-new life, completely different than before. The view of the secular world is that this is impossible... that "people never change" any more than a "tiger can change his stripes." But even as Jesus transformed the murderer Saul, into the mighty Apostle Paul... Christ continues today to save and transform the lives of those who come to Him. *"...if anyone is in Christ, he is a new creation; old things have passed away; behold, all things have become new" (2 Corinthians 5:17).*

Some think that it's unrealistic, or that it builds false hopes, to encourage persons to pray for miraculous things.

39

However, I don't find that viewpoint in the New Testament... just the opposite. The scriptures recount story after story of faith-building miracles, along with the repeated encouragements by Jesus and His Apostles, to believe for the impossible. Jesus said, *"...Have faith in God. For assuredly, I say to you, whoever says to this mountain, 'Be removed and be cast into the sea,' and does not doubt in his heart, but believes that those things he says will be done, he will have whatever he says. Therefore, I say to you, whatever things you ask when you pray, believe that you receive them, and you will have them"* (Mark 11:22-24).

Tom's remarkable recovery over many months was nothing short of a miraculous answer to prayer. But now I want to share an astonishing instantaneous miracle that I watched the Lord perform a few years back.

An Instantaneous Miracle

While pastoring a church in California, I invited an evangelist to come, who was especially known for healings and spiritual gifts that accompanied his ministry. During the week he preached in our nightly meetings, and I assisted him in praying for folks who came to the altars for various needs. And by the week's end, dozens had testified to having received healing or other results from prayer.

Finally, in the last service, a woman brought her elderly mother to the altar for prayer. I knew them both, and had previously visited and prayed with the mom. She was severely disabled and could barely walk, because one leg was a few inches shorter than the other.

When the evangelist heard this, he asked one of our elders

to get a chair for the mother, and lift both her legs onto another chair facing her. When that was done, everyone could see that her left leg was considerably shorter than the other. It was a very moving moment for the congregation to see her disability, and many began praying quietly that the Lord might bring her a miracle.

However, instead of approaching the woman to pray for her, as he had done with others, the evangelist pulled away and prayed privately for a few moments. I waited for him to return, so that I could assist him in praying. But I was surprised when he didn't, and made an unexpected statement instead.

Speaking into his mic so all could hear, he said, *"Pastor, the Lord has shown me that He wants to use you to pray for this sister today, both to help her and to do something special in your life. In times past, He used your prayers of faith and authority in mighty ways, and He wants you to return to that kind of praying... so He can use you in even greater ways."*

Needless to say, I was stunned. I wasn't prepared to hear a prophetic word that involved me... nor was I expecting to pray alone for this disabled person. I didn't know how to respond, except to turn toward the woman and prepare to pray for her. But the evangelist interrupted once more, leaving me speechless by what he said next.

"Pastor, there's no need to do anything else," He said. *"Just point your hand toward her, and in faith, command her shorter leg to 'come forth.'"*

"What did he say again?! I'm just supposed to command her leg... to what?" I was completely astounded. I certainly didn't doubt that the Lord could heal this woman, but the

41

evangelist was forecasting the certainty of an imminent miracle... one that I'd never seen happen before, and that the Lord was supposed to use "me" to bring it about!

At this point, every eye turned toward me, to see what I was going to do. For a moment I was tempted to think that the evangelist had gone bonkers. However, I had seen this man's genuineness with God, and observed true gifts of the Holy Spirit operating through him. I was confident he wasn't trying to do anything weird, but had every expectation that we were about to witness a demonstration of God's mighty power. And so, I quickly decided, that's what I would believe too.

I first crouched down maybe 24 inches or so from the elderly mom's short leg, to get a close view of anything that happened, while one of our elders stood watching at my side. The woman sat still in the chair, listening and observing, while her daughter stood behind with hands on her shoulders. The congregation grew silent, then without touching her, I lifted my hand, pointed at her left leg and spoke out with an authoritative tone. *"In the name of Jesus... Come Forth!"*

At the precise moment that I said this, her leg suddenly launched forward in a smooth fluid motion, as though a hydraulic lever had been pulled. While she remained motionless in the chair, her leg continued growing out from the sleeve of her slacks, about a half inch per second, until it reached the same length as the other. It was the most astonishing thing I've ever seen!

While we began praising and thanking the Lord, I looked up briefly at the elder beside me... he was still staring at the leg in amazement. Those sitting near the front who had seen this, were also stunned... as was I. Not that I doubted that God could or would do such a thing, but that I actually saw the process of it happening before my eyes. I was also deeply amazed and humbled that the Lord would use me, to command her leg to grow out... a confirmation of the prophetic word given to me from the evangelist.

And the thing that blew me away me most, was the precise "timing" of what I witnessed. It was neither a millisecond before, nor a millisecond afterward... but at the exact moment that I uttered the words *"Come forth."* Her leg responded instantly, without delay or lag, growing out at the same smooth constant rate.

I'd never seen anything like it... the close-up observation of a miracle as it happened in real-time. Of course, I've prayed for throngs of people, and have heard the testimonies of many who received healings or blessings. But I had never witnessed the actual "process" of any of these things as they occurred.

It had been a long time since I'd seen such marvelous answers to prayers in our services. And it appeared that God meant for this miracle, to not only bless this dear woman, but also to speak personally to me... to reawaken my faith, and draw me to a deeper place of prayer and humility.

The miracle did exactly that, and literally changed my life... however not immediately. It took a long time to ponder and process what I had witnessed. But I eventually heard the Lord telling me to humble myself before Him with a lifestyle of prayer with fasting, so that He could bring that same kind of anointing and use my prayers in greater ways for Him. This was actually something I had felt the Lord drawing me to for a long time, but unfortunately, I had hesitated and procrastinated.

So finally coming to terms with what the Lord was leading me to do, I began this new regimen of prayer... which revolutionized my life and ministry. I had fasted with prayer many times in previous years, but only for brief durations and on rare occasions. Now I had fresh insight as to its importance, how it benefited me spiritually, and why God was calling me to do this consistently.

Since that time, prayer with fasting has become a regular practice, and my relationship with the Lord has grown more intimate. I hear His direction and guidance more clearly, and I have a greater passion to please and honor Him with my life. This is really what prayer with fasting is about... "spiritual intimacy." Not merely to get answers to prayers. It's a spiritual discipline to submit and "humble self" before the Lord, to allow Him and the influence of His Spirit to increase, while the influence of our self-willed flesh is decreased.

And as this new spiritual realignment has unfolded in me, the Lord also began bringing a greater anointing upon both my wife and I, and extending His Spiritual gifts through our ministry. We have already seen greater and immediate results from our prayers, and have no doubt that we'll again see the Lord perform similar and greater kinds of miracles in the days ahead.

Andrew Murray once wrote, *"Beware in your prayers, above everything else, of limiting God, not only by unbelief, but by fancying that you know what He can do. Expect unexpected things, above all that we ask or think."*[1]

When praying for what seems like impossible things, consider these faith-building passages:

"Jesus said to him, If you can believe, all things are possible to him who believes" (Mark 9:23).

"And whatever you ask in My name, that I will do, that the Father may be glorified in the Son. If you ask anything in My name, I will do it" (John 14:13-14).

"But without faith it is impossible to please Him, for he who comes to God must believe that He is, and that He is a rewarder of those who diligently seek Him" (Hebrews 11:6).

"So Jesus said to them, ...for assuredly, I say to you, if you have faith as a mustard seed, you will say to this mountain, 'Move from here to there,' and it will move; and nothing will be impossible for you. However, this kind does not go out except by prayer and fasting" (Matthew 17:20-21).

"Again I say to you that if two of you agree on earth concerning anything that they ask, it will be done for them by My Father in heaven" (Matthew 18:19).

"Keep on asking, and you will receive what you ask for. Keep on seeking, and you will find. Keep on knocking, and the door will be opened to you. For everyone who asks, receives. Everyone who seeks, finds. And to everyone who knocks, the door will be opened. You parents if your children ask for a loaf of bread, do you give them a stone instead? Or if they ask for a fish, do you give them a snake? Of course not! So if you sinful people know how to give good gifts to your children, how much more will your

*heavenly Father give good gifts to those who ask him"
(Matthew 7:7-11 NLT).*

[1] *Waiting on God, Andrew Murray, 1898*

13. Why Does the Bible Say to Pray in Secret?

Jesus taught that spiritual acts, such as charitable giving
and prayer, should be done in secret so to affirm the
genuineness of our motives toward God. In other words,
such things done in private are to assure that God alone
knows about them... so that our motives can remain pure,
seeking only to please and honor Him, rather than seeking
recognition or admiration from man.

Jesus said, *"Watch out! Don't do your good deeds publicly,
to be admired by others, for you will lose the reward from
your Father in heaven. When you give to someone in need,
don't do as the hypocrites do—blowing trumpets in the
synagogues and streets to call attention to their acts of
charity! I tell you the truth, they have received all the
reward they will ever get. But when you give to someone in
need, don't let your left hand know what your right hand
is doing. Give your gifts in private, and your Father, who
sees everything, will reward you. When you pray, don't be
like the hypocrites who love to pray publicly on street
corners and in the synagogues where everyone can see
them. I tell you the truth, that is all the reward they will
ever get. But when you pray, go away by yourself, shut the
door behind you, and pray to your Father in private. Then
your Father, who sees everything, will reward you"
(Matthew 6:1-6 NLT).*

Without a doubt, fervent secret prayer, combined with tenacious faith and perseverance, plays an important role to effective prayer. The late Leonard Ravenhill, one of the past great apostles of prayer and revival, once wrote, *"Do you know what the secret of praying is? Praying in secret... You can't show off when the door's shut and nobody's there."*[1]

Not only does such private or secluded prayer serve to validate our sincerity toward God, but it can also help us focus more clearly on God alone, without the distractions of other cares or thoughts. God places special value on seeking Him wholeheartedly, and assures that such diligence will be rewarded. *"And you will seek Me and find Me, when you search for Me with all your heart" (Jeremiah 29:13).* Andrew Murray put it this way, *"Shut the world out, withdraw from all worldly thoughts and occupations, and shut yourself in alone with God, to pray to Him in secret. Let this be your chief object in prayer, to realize the presence of your heavenly Father."*[2]

Praying in secret also conveys the idea of a close and personal relationship... opening yourself, and trusting God with the most intimate contents of your heart. It involves confiding your deepest feelings, thoughts or concerns to Him, the things you've never shared with anyone else. Trusting Him with your secrets, your hidden thoughts... and confessing your sins, flaws or shortcomings, are all a part of trusting and loving Him *"with all your heart, with all your soul, and with all your mind" (Matthew 22:37).* This type of closeness with the Lord, is probably what the psalmist was referring to when he referred to the "secret place" of fellowship with God. *"He who dwells in the secret place of the Most High Shall abide under the shadow of the Almighty" (Psalms 91:1).*

This doesn't mean that all prayer must be secret or private. Instances of public or corporate prayer are also valid and important. Besides praying much in seclusion, such as often going up into the mountains to pray alone *(Matthew 14:23)*, Jesus prayed openly in many instances too, for the benefit of those who would hear *(John 11:41-43)*. He also taught for believers to pray together in agreement on particular matters, which would not be possible unless they vocalize their prayers openly or are aware of what each are praying. *"If two of you agree here on earth concerning anything you ask, my Father in heaven will do it for you" (Matthew 18:19 NLT).*

Obviously, there will be some prayers best kept secret only between you and God, but even your public prayers must always consist of the same genuineness and wholeheartedness toward Him, not for the sake of show or to impress anyone with your eloquence or supposed spirituality.

[1] *Prayer, Leonard Ravenhill, 1995*
[2] *Daily Secrets of Christian Living, Andrew Murray, 1917*

14. Why Don't We Hear More About Miracles?

Probably because you've not been listening to the right sources. I hear amazing testimonies about miracles and answered prayers quite often, primarily because I'm involved with ministry to encourage prayer and faith, and am usually in churches and places where people are encouraged to believe God's promises. The secular news media seldom reports such things... but whenever they can't avoid it, it's usually only reported from a skeptical or ridiculing perspective.

But even though more miraculous answers to prayer occur than what we often hear about in the public, it's also true that they are not commonplace or as frequent as they once were in America. It's not because God has changed or has ceased from doing such things... but because our society has largely regressed away from believing God and His Word. Obviously, where there is little faith or openness to the Holy Spirit, miracles and amazing answers to prayer will be equally as scarce.

When I was a young preacher of the Gospel, it became obvious to me that America had drifted far away from God and the Christian principles on which our nation was founded. But it was not until I had an opportunity to preach and minister overseas, that I had something with which to compare... to realize the depth of unbelief that has permeated our modern culture.

During a missionary tour to the Philippines in the mid 1980's, I became impressed by the people's openness and eagerness to accept the Gospel message wherever I would minister. I would usually preach in two or three places daily with very little or no advance promotion, yet regardless where I went, crowds came and responded enthusiastically to the Word of God. This was a stark contrast between similar meetings I held in the states.

And especially remarkable to me, was their simple faith to believe the preaching of God's Word, and their willingness to welcome the presence of the Holy Spirit. In just a matter of days, scores of souls had been saved in our meetings. And most amazing, were the numbers of those who testified of healings and miracles as I laid on my hands and prayed.

While I have always believed in praying for the sick, back in the U.S. it seemed that results from our prayers had usually been mixed, with only "occasional" testimonies of healings here and there. However, in this third-world nation, something had shifted dramatically. The greater percentage of those I prayed for, claimed to receive healing. And usually not from some minor malady like a headache... but scary things, like malaria, tuberculosis, blindness, deafness... including some diseases that I thought no longer existed.

In one village where I preached, they setup a makeshift podium in the middle of the main intersection, and that evening, crowds filled the narrow streets in all directions to hear me speak. I was shocked by the numbers of persons who were saved and healed... and by those who lingered even after the meetings were concluded. This and similar responses occurred most everywhere I ministered, even when I spoke for a chapel service at their largest university, the Polytechnic University of the Philippines in Manila. At the conclusion of my Gospel message, I gave an invitation through an interpreter for students to stand and receive Christ as their savior. I was surprised when nearly the entire audience stood, so I asked the interpreter to repeat my request, to make sure they understood. At this, the body of students remained standing... as I led virtually all of them in the sinner's prayer.

And just when I was tempted to think that I had transformed into some kind of super preacher, I experienced a reality check and was reminded that I was no different than the day I boarded the plane in San Francisco. The only change was the place where I was preaching. The people, the environment, their openness to

God's Word and His Spirit, was somehow different than our U.S. audiences. My typically average preaching and ministry was being received and responded to in remarkable ways that I never experienced.

For whatever reason, it appeared that unbelief, skepticism or cynicism was not as ingrained into the Filipino culture. While usually the first response of a Westerner is to "question" the things they hear, the Filipinos are more inclined to "believe." Some think of this as gullibility, but I'm convinced that this is actually the more normal disposition toward the Gospel message. Belief would be more common in our society, without the layers of diversion, suspicion and cynicism that has saturated American-Western society.

Consequently, the scarcity of miracles, wonders and answers to prayer in America has mainly to do with unbelief. Our society, even the majority of our churches and clergy, have regressed away from believing and trusting in God and His Word. Sin, wickedness, immorality rules our nation simply because people neither believe in the consequences of sin, nor the rewards of righteousness as described in God's Word. And neither do they have faith to appreciate or procure the marvelous benefits that come through prayer and trusting God.

To witness and experience more of the miraculous nature of God, faith must be built up, and the Holy Spirit's presence must be welcomed to fill our lives and churches. This will require believers to dwell more upon God's Word and spiritual things, than the things of this world. Instead of spending all our time seeking entertainment and worldly amusements, we'll need to sacrifice time to pray, fast, worship, and meditate on scripture. And then God's

Spiritual gifts will begin to flow, and faith will begin to surge, bringing a desire and ability to believe God for the impossible.

We all have prayed that this sort of thirst for God and righteous will return and flourish again someday in America. But it will probably not happen until Americans suffer the consequences for their sin and godlessness, and have nowhere else to turn for help. If or when that happens, God will be there waiting... ready to forgive truly repentant souls, to restore them back to His love and favor.

15. Why Should I Be Careful About What I Pray For?

This old adage, *"be careful what you pray for,"* has been quoted in church circles as long as I can remember. However, while it's always good advice to consider our motivations and the consequences of anything we pray and ask God for, we should also be aware that God doesn't answer prayers indiscriminately, or simply on the basis of selfish, sinful or careless whims. Generally speaking, the Lord doesn't comply with requests that are contrary to His will. The Bible says that God cannot be tempted to do anything that is evil or unrighteous *(James 1:13)*, and that the prayers He listens to, are those that conform to His will. *"Now this is the confidence that we have in Him, that if we ask anything according to His will, He hears us" (1 John 5:14).*

Fortunately, God takes all things into consideration, and filters some prayers, because people can sometimes ask for some incredibly foolish and unscriptural things. I regret to say that in my past, especially as a young believer, I asked for some pretty stupid things... which I'm so glad didn't come to pass! Even the greatest men of God have at times prayed ridiculous prayers that God simply ignored... such as when Moses, Elijah and Jonah each asked the Lord to kill themselves *(Numbers 11:13-15, 1 Kings 19:3-4, Jonah 4:1-4)*. (Hey, it was pretty tough to be a prophet!)

And we can't forget the time when Jesus wasn't welcomed by a Samaritan village... so James and John asked if He'd like them to "call fire down from heaven" to destroy them *(Luke 9:54)*. What were these guys thinking?! Can't you just imagine the fiasco that could ensue if people had unrestricted access to answered prayers? The sudden surge of lottery winners, or perhaps a rise in vengeful lightning strikes!

Sometimes I hear people make bogus claims that God answered some obviously wicked or unholy prayer request. Unfortunately, God is often falsely credited (or blamed) for answering such prayers or doing things that He had no part in.

For instance, some years ago I knew a preacher who received a letter containing a bizarre prayer request. It was from a woman who despised her husband and was asking the pastor to pray for him to die. The preacher was shocked! She promised that after her husband was dead, she would give half of his life insurance proceeds to the church.

The pastor was utterly stunned to see such a wicked prayer request. But a week or so later, before he was able to compose a reply to rebuke this woman, he got another letter from her. This one "thanked him" for his prompt prayers and included a check! She explained that her husband had promptly died like she had asked. Even more alarmed to see this, the preacher immediately returned the check, making sure she understood that he did not nor would ever pray for such an evil thing.

So, did God answer this woman's prayers for her husband to die? Of course not. The poor man was likely already on his deathbed and would have expired anyway. But, sadly, this woman's story was spread far and wide, claiming falsely that God answered her prayers to kill her husband. However, as we've said, the Bible tells us that God doesn't answer prayers that are evil or which contradict His will... nor does He hear the prayers of evil people. *"Now we know that God does not hear sinners; but if anyone is a worshiper of God and does His will, He hears him"* (John 9:31).

Figuring out the difference between good and evil prayer requests is generally not hard, but determining God's will in other matters is not always simple. The Bible clearly explains many aspects of God's desires, which helps us to know how to pray.... but there are also other matters, not directly addressed in scripture, with which we may wrestle to find His perfect will. We also may experience times of great difficulty, trials or tribulations, that may cloud our understanding of His desires for our life, or which seem to lead us in other directions. Under such circumstances, we may find ourselves struggling to grasp His will or to pray for the right kind of things.

These are the kinds of circumstances to especially use caution with what you pray for. God already knows your needs, and how best to intervene in your life and circumstances... if you will trust Him to work out the details. But people will sometimes panic or get in a hurry, or may try to "dictate" or tell God how to fix their problems or what's best for themselves. In many instances, this has hindered their prayers from being answered at all. But on some occasions... He may allow some persistent prayers to be answered from His "permissive" will, although perhaps not from His "perfect" will.

This idea of differing levels of God's will is something that theologians have sometimes disagreed on, based mostly on contrasting interpretations of this passage, *"...be transformed by the renewing of your mind, that you may prove what is that good and acceptable and perfect will of God" (Romans 12:2)*. The Apostle Paul was explaining that the minds of believers need renewed by God's Word and His Holy Spirit, in order to understand what pleases the Lord. Some Christians feel that Paul was combining adjectives here to offer a "single description" of God's will... that it is "good, acceptable and perfect." Others, however, think that he was describing separate graduating levels that meet God's approval... the "good," OR the "acceptable," OR the "perfect will of God."

Regardless of the meaning here, experience suggests that God does indeed sometimes allow something less than His "perfect plan," and will occasionally apply prayers toward a permissible or acceptable plan "B." AND there are times that, for whatever reason... perhaps to teach a lesson to those who are defiant and should know better, He will even grant persistent requests that seem to conflict with His will.

But of course, **whenever persons pursue anything less than God's perfect will, it will almost always come with a cost of unexpected consequences or**

regrets, such as with the Israelites in the wilderness, who pleaded with Moses to give them meat when they became discontent with the Lord's provision of manna. So, the Lord sent them great hordes of quail... until many literally gorged themselves to death *(Numbers 11:1-31).*

In another instance, despite the Lord's will to the contrary, Israel kept demanding a king. So, God eventually relented and gave them a king... Saul, who was a disastrous leader with many problems, and who they eventually disdained *(1 Samuel 8:1-21).* Those who go to God with the intent of insisting on "their own plans," may sometimes get what they ask, but sometimes also suffer undesirable repercussions.

The better approach is to always seek God's perfect will, even as Jesus did in the Garden of Gethsemane, during the most stressful moments of His earthly life. Although Jesus knew His purpose in coming to the earth, to give His life for the sins of the world, His flesh struggled to accept the reality of the suffering and death that was approaching. His pleading prayer was, *"Father, if it is Your will, take this cup away from Me..." (Luke 22:42a).*

Of course, for Jesus to willingly give His life for our sins, it was not possible to avoid the torment and brutal crucifixion He was about to face. But His humanity asked this anyway... while at the same time, surrendering Himself to the will of the Heavenly Father. *"...nevertheless, not My will, but Yours, be done" (Luke 22:42b).*

What we learn is that regardless of whatever hopes or desires that we have for ourselves, the bottom line is that we should always pray in such a way to surrender ourselves to "accept His will above our own." By all means, take your burdens, needs and desires to the Lord... but with the objective to trust "His perfect plan" for your life, even if it may be contrary to your wishes. *"Not My will, but Yours, be done."* James even suggested that this kind of assent should always overrule our words or thoughts about any of our possible plans or ambitions, saying, *"...you ought to say, If the Lord wills, we shall live and do this or that" (James 4:15).*

Fortunately, if sincere believers make mistakes in praying for the wrong things, God will usually "edit or revise" such requests, either by not responding... or by answering the prayer in some other way that fits into His will, but also meets our need. Yet the better way is to always seek God's perfect will from the beginning. Instead of trying to twist God's arm to bless our own plans or ideas, seek out and find "His" plans and ideas, that already have His blessing. God will never hesitate from answering the prayer for those things that He already wants for you.

16. Can Prayer Change God's Mind or Will?

This is a common question I sometimes hear, but really deals with whether God can "change a situation" by answering what might seem to be an impossible prayer request. Or perhaps whether He can intervene in or alter an irreversible situation.

Be assured that prayer "does change things," by inviting God's help with our needs or problems. Since He is "omnipotent" (all-powerful), He has an unlimited ability to do impossible things when people are willing to believe

Him and the promises of His Word. *"For with God nothing will be impossible" (Luke 1:37).*

However, prayer really doesn't involve changing the Lord's mind about anything. Although in past times God has expressed regret at man's sinful choices or actions *(Genesis 6:7, 1 Samuel 15:11)*, numerous Bible passages tell us that God "does not change" *(Malachi 3:6)*. In fact, He doesn't "vary in the slightest" way *(James 1:17)*, and unlike man, doesn't change his mind *(Numbers 23:19)*. It even says that His word is *"forever... settled in heaven" (Psalms 119:89).*

After all, what need is there for God to change His mind? He is "omniscient" (all-knowing), and already knows the future, along with every detail about every situation... so nothing comes as a surprise to Him. He knows our needs, what decisions we will make, and has maintained a long-standing plan in place for each of us before we were born. *"...just as He chose us in Him before the foundation of the world, that we should be holy and without blame before Him in love" (Ephesians 1:4).*

Yet, while there are instances in Bible history where it "appears" that God changes His mind, in reality these deal with man's change in his attitude or faith toward God. The Lord already has a foreordained plan for those who submit to His will... but also has other alternate plans for those who make other choices.

Such was the case when God answered King Hezekiah's prayers for healing. After the Lord warned him that he was going to die, Hezekiah surrendered his attitude and humbled himself before the Lord, who then added fifteen more years to his life, *"I have heard your prayer, I have*

seen your tears; surely I will heal you..." (2 Kings 20:5).
(See the full text 2 Kings 20:1-7) However, while God's
plan for Hezekiah changed, it was not a change of His
mind or will, but rather a change in Hezekiah and His
disposition toward God.

God's mind is already made up about good and wonderful
things He wants for His people, which He declares in His
Word. But He cannot implement such high ideals in man's
affairs without his cooperation and invitation through
prayer. This doesn't mean that God's power is limited or
impotent in any way, but rather that He has placed "self-
imposed" limitations on His intervention into man's free
will. This is a large part of what Jesus meant when He
told his disciples (and us all) that we must pray that our
Father's will *"...be done on earth as it is in heaven" (Luke*
11:2).

It is God's will and desire to bless and do many wonderful
things for people, but He needs us to submit ourselves to
His plan... to follow Him, and to pray and believe for His
will to be done. Unfortunately, because people, even
believers, are often rebellious and self-willed, they are
unable to attain God's best plan for their lives.

Another example can be seen in the story of Jonah, the
prophet who rebelled at God and was swallowed by a great
fish. After he repented and was spewed up from the belly
of the fish, he reluctantly obeyed the Lord by going to
Nineveh and proclaiming God's impending judgment. The
Bible says, *"...Jonah began to enter the city on the first*
day's walk. Then he cried out and said, Yet forty days, and
Nineveh shall be overthrown!" (Jonah 3:4).

Destruction was never God's will or desire for the people of Nineveh, but was the unfortunate reality of their own choices. Unless "they" changed their minds and repented of their sin, God's judgment would be unavoidable.

And how surprised Jonah was by their reaction to his warning. Not only did the people believe him, but they responded with humility and repentance. The king even proclaimed a nation-wide fast to call upon on the Lord, and implored the people to turn from evil and from violence.... with the hope that God might "change His mind" about Nineveh's destruction. (Wow, is this what's needed in America or what?)

The king said, *"But let man and beast be covered with sackcloth, and cry mightily to God; yes, let every one turn from his evil way and from the violence that is in his hands. Who can tell if God will turn and relent, and turn away from His fierce anger, so that we may not perish? Then God saw their works, that they turned from their evil way; and God relented from the disaster that He had said He would bring upon them, and He did not do it"* (Jonah 3:8-10).

From the perspective of the Ninevites, it "appeared" that the Lord changed His mind, however the only thing that changed was the hearts of the people, who repented once they knew judgment was coming for sure. God's will is already established for those who do evil... and is also established or for those who repent and follow the Lord. He doesn't need to make any adjustments. His mind is already made up.

The same is true for us today. God's will and desire is not for anyone to be lost or to spend eternity in the lake of

fire, but unfortunately that fate awaits those who choose
to reject the redemptive gift of Jesus Christ. *"The Lord
is... not willing that any should perish but that all should
come to repentance" (2 Peter 3:9).* Repentance means to
"change one's mind," and is the only way to avert this
eternal tragedy... to reject a life of sin and choose to
believe and follow Jesus Christ.

So instead of trying to persuade God to submit to our will,
what we need is to submit our will to His. Rather than
praying to change God's mind, we actually need to pray
for "our" heart and mind to change, to come into
submission and alignment to His will and desire for our
life. This is really the key to finding God's favor, blessings
and getting answers to prayer. As Jesus said in His prayer
at Gethsemane, *"...nevertheless not my will, but thine, be
done" (Luke 22:42 KJV).*

All too often, people spin their wheels, trying to get God to
bless something that's not a part of His plan or will, but as
I've shared before, you'll not find it so difficult to attain
God's favor for those things He wants for you. And believe
it or not, His desires for you, always exceed your own... if
you will just trust Him, and yield your life to Him. The
Bible says that when it becomes your pleasure to obey and
please the Lord, He will fulfill your heart's desires.
*"Delight yourself also in the Lord, And He shall give you
the desires of your heart. Commit your way to the Lord,
Trust also in Him, And He shall bring it to pass" (Psalms
37:4-5).*

*"If you abide in Me, and My words abide in you, you will
ask what you desire, and it shall be done for you" (John
15:7)*

"Eye has not seen, nor ear heard, Nor have entered into the heart of man The things which <u>God has prepared</u> for those who love Him" (1 Corinthians 2:9).

17. Why Pray When I Don't Need Anything?

Because prayer is the way a Christian engages in fellowship and communication with the Lord. In other words, prayer is necessary in order to have a relationship with God. Prayer, along with your study and meditation upon God's Word, are the means that He uses to lead and guide you, to infuse His spiritual strength and presence into your life.

Even if you are unaware of any personal needs or problems to pray about, you always need more of the Lord's presence in your life... which comes through prayer. You can be praying for growth in your spiritual relationship with God, strength to rise above future temptations or trials, for your relationships with your family. You can pray for energy and passion in your career, the wisdom to make right and wise decisions, your service or ministry to your church, or the opportunity to be used of God to bless or encourage others in your life.

And besides praying for your own personal needs or relationship with Christ, there are a gazillion other people, situations or problems that also need your prayers. In his book, *Effective Prayer Life*, author Chuck Smith, founder of Calvary Chapel, said *"Prayer is the most important activity a born-again Christian can perform. It should head your list of priorities, for certainly the world around us desperately needs prayer."*[1]

Paul told Timothy that prayers should be made for everyone, and especially for kings and those in authority... which would include our government leaders, councilmen, senators, congressmen, governors and even the president. *"Therefore, I exhort first of all that supplications, prayers, intercessions, and giving of thanks be made for all men, for kings and all who are in authority, that we may lead a quiet and peaceable life in all godliness and reverence"* (1 Timothy 2:1-2).

And we never have to look far to find more things to pray for. Pray for the salvation of your family, friends or coworkers... and for the variety of other problems or challenges they may be facing. Pray for your pastor and church leaders, for missionaries and evangelists preaching the Gospel locally and abroad, for persecuted Christians, many of whom are being tortured or murdered for Christ at this very moment.

Pray for the homeless, the fatherless, widows, the poor, for the safety and well-being of police, firemen, as well as our military men and women serving abroad. Pray for the help, encouragement and rescue of people who have suffered natural and man-made disasters.

Pray for the healing of racial and political conflicts in our nation, for a lasting peace in Israel, the Middle-East and all nations, and for an end of the human tragedies caused by the evils of terrorism. These are some of the most dangerous times the world has ever seen... and people everywhere need to be in prayer for the nations.

You also need to pray for revival to come to your community, as well as our nation and the world. Pray especially for America, which desperately needs a spiritual awakening... which can only come through prayer and repentance. *"if My people who are called by My name will humble themselves, and pray and seek My face, and turn from their wicked ways, then I will hear from heaven, and will forgive their sin and heal their land' (2 Chronicles 7:14).*

Think that your prayers for such big things can't make a difference? Think again. Jesus actually taught each of us to pray *"His kingdom come and will be done on earth"* *(Matthew 6:10).* To ask for His will to come upon the earth certainly sounds like a challenging and near-impossible thing, but He responds to such prayers daily, by intervening in the affairs of the world and in the lives of millions who ask.

E.M. Bounds, one of the most prolific authors on the subject of prayer in the 19th century, said *"God shapes the world by prayer. The more prayer there is in the world the better the world will be, the mightier the forces against evil."*[2]

[1] *Effective Prayer Life, Chuck Smith, Calvary Chapel, 1980*
[2]*Purpose in Prayer, E.M. Bounds, 1921*

18. What Should I Say When I Pray?
(The Lord's Prayer)

Approach the Heavenly Father in prayer through the name of Jesus. Speak to Him in your own words, with humility, love and respect. Eloquence or religious-sounding "thees" and "thous" are not necessary... just be yourself, talk to Him with love and esteem, like your best friend. He is your Father, your Creator, the source of all blessings who loves you more than anyone else in the world.

The scriptures also contain many examples of prayers that can become the framework for your own... or which you can pray as your own words. Many times I simply pray the scriptures, or recite the words of Jesus' prayers from the Gospels. I especially cherish the prayers of David found in the Psalms.

One of the most remarkable prayers you will ever read, is found in the 51st Psalm, David's remorseful prayer when he finally repented of his adultery and murder *(2 Samuel 11 – 12)*. When the Lord has convicted my heart of sin or disobedience in the past, I have sometimes recited and prayed these words as my own: *"Create in me a clean heart, O God, And renew a steadfast spirit within me. Do not cast me away from Your presence, And do not take Your Holy Spirit from me. Restore to me the joy of Your salvation, And uphold me by Your generous Spirit" (Psalms 51:10-12).*

This and his other humble prayers and expressions of worship in the Psalms, helps us to understand why David was called a man after God's heart *(Acts 13:22)*. He was referred to as such, not because he was perfect in any way, but because he humbled himself and repented remorsefully for his sins when confronted and convicted by the Lord.

And especially helpful, is the tutorial that Jesus gave to His disciples when they asked Him to teach them to pray. *"Now it came to pass, as He was praying in a certain place, when He ceased, that one of His disciples said to Him, Lord, teach us to pray, as John also taught his disciples" (Luke 11:1).*

I'm sure when Jesus heard this, He was thrilled to respond and give his disciples an example to use when they prayed, which we all came to know as the "Lord's Prayer" *(Matthew 6:5-15, Luke 11:1-4)*. However, before offering that, He emphasized that prayer was a type of personal, intimate communion with God, not something for "show" for man's benefit, nor a matter of simply repeating or chanting words.

Jesus said, *"And when you pray, you shall not be like the hypocrites. For they love to pray standing in the synagogues and on the corners of the streets, that they may be seen by men. Assuredly, I say to you, they have their reward. But you, when you pray, go into your room, and when you have shut your door, pray to your Father who is in the secret place; and your Father who sees in secret will reward you openly. And when you pray, do not use vain repetitions as the heathen do. For they think that they will be heard for their many words. Therefore, do not be like them. For your Father knows the things you have need of before you ask Him"* *(Matthew 6:5-8)*.

After these remarks, Jesus then presented what became known as the Lord's Prayer, a text regarded as sacred to generations of Christians, intended not only to be venerated, recited and re-prayed, but primarily to be used as a "pattern" or a "tutorial" for our own prayerful thoughts and words.

The Lord's Prayer

Jesus said, **"In this manner, therefore, pray: Our Father in heaven, Hallowed be Your name. Your kingdom come. Your will be done On earth as it is in heaven. Give us this day our daily bread. And** *forgive us our debts, As we forgive our debtors. And do not lead us into temptation, But deliver us from the evil one. For Yours is the kingdom and the power and the glory forever. Amen" (Matthew 6:9-13).*

Many truths can be gleaned from the Lord's Prayer, but Jesus emphasized at least five important patterns for believers to maintain in their ongoing prayer life:

(1) Pray with an attitude of humility and reverence toward our Heavenly Father. *"Our Father in heaven, Hallowed be Your name." (Matthew 6:9).* Our God is not some stone-faced lifeless idol, but a person, our "Father," with whom we have divine relationship as our spiritual parent. To be allowed to come into the presence of our Creator is an incredibly humbling privilege. His name is to be "hallowed," that is, to be humbly revered and respected as sacred, special or holy. We also must remember that Heaven is the destination of where your prayers are directed, not merely the earth for the hearing of men.

(2) Pray for our Father's will and justice to reign on earth, as it does in Heaven. *"Your will be done on earth as it is in heaven" (Matthew 6:10).* Simple observation shows us that our world contains much depravity, pain and misery, unlike the realm of goodness and perfection that exists in Heaven. But as believers and "citizens" of Heaven, the Lord has given us the right and responsibility to pray and bring those blessings of Heaven to needs upon the Earth.

(3) Pray for the Lord to meet our daily needs and provisions. *"Give us this day our daily bread" (Matthew 6:11).* Contrary to what some people think, your Heavenly

Father is delighted when you rely on Him, and trust Him to be your provider of blessings and provisions.

(4) Pray for daily forgiveness of sin, as we also forgive others for their sins against us. *"And forgive us our debts, As we forgive our debtors" (Matthew 6:12).* This is the daily practice of true believers, who live and walk in a spirit of repentance and humility. We all make our share of mistakes on a daily basis, as do others who often trespass against us. So daily we must forgive, as well as be forgiven.

(5) Pray for the Lord's continual guidance and avoidance from Satan's snares. *"And do not lead us into temptation, But deliver us from the evil one..." (Luke 11:4).* Our adversary, the Devil, is a reality that we will always contend with as followers of Christ, and we need our Father's daily continued guidance and protection to bypass or overcome the hindrances he may interject.

19. How or Where Should I Pray?

Closing one's eyes and/or kneeling have long been traditional postures for prayer, but it really doesn't matter. We see instances when Jesus knelt and prayed *(Luke 22:41),* but on other occasions He looked toward heaven as He prayed *(John 17:1).* He also referred to standing while praying *(Luke 18:11, Mark 11:25),* and even prostrated himself during His prayer in the Garden of Gethsemane. *"He went a little farther and fell on His face, and prayed, saying, 'O My Father, if it is possible, let this cup pass from Me; nevertheless, not as I will, but as You will.'" (Matthew 26:39).*

Praying at an altar in a church is another popular tradition, which has been especially meaningful to me personally. But the fact is, you can pray anyplace. Altars or churches are often viewed as sacred places that may help remind us of God's presence and inspire us to pray, but in the New Testament the Holy Spirit is not limited to a building or a particular site or object. The scripture says that YOU are the temple of His Holy Spirit *(1 Corinthians 3:16),* and He is available anywhere you are, to hear the prayers of your heart.

While there will be moments when others will hear us pray, or during moments we pray openly or publicly with other believers, most of our prayer life should be secret and private just between you and the Lord. Jesus doesn't specify any particular place, but illustrated this as going into a secluded room and shutting the door... or into a "closet" as the King James translation says. *"But thou, when thou prayest, enter into thy closet, and when thou hast shut thy door, pray to thy Father which is in secret; and thy Father which seeth in secret shall reward thee openly" (Matthew 6:6 KJV).*

Finding such a private place or opportunity can sometimes be difficult in our busy world. I discovered this to be the case after I first became a Christian. Prayer had become a big part of my relationship with Jesus, but I often struggled to find moments of privacy during my work day. I tried to spend many of my breaks and lunch times in prayer, but to do so I had to either seclude myself in my car, go for a walk outside, or find a private place inside my workplace. This was often difficult, and sometimes made for awkward moments. On a few occasions, fellow workers stumbled across me praying in a vacant office, in the men's room, or even in the janitor's closet. One instance was especially humorous, when a fellow worker opened the door and flipped on the light to a tiny maintenance closet, where they were startled to find me talking to "someone" among the mops and buckets!

But even when seclusion can't be found, you can still talk to the Lord beneath your breath, or even in your thoughts, as you go about your duties. Billy Graham said, *"You can pray anytime, anywhere. Washing dishes, digging ditches, working in the office, in the shop, on the athletic field, even in prison -- you can pray and know God hears!"[1]*

[1] *Peace with God: The Secret of Happiness, Billy Graham, 1953*

20. Who Do I Pray to... God, Jesus or the Holy Spirit?

It's a common practice for believers to address their prayers primarily to God the Heavenly Father, through the name of His son, Jesus Christ. This is why Christian prayers are generally concluded by saying, *"In Jesus name."* Jesus said *"whatever you ask the Father in My name He will give you" (John 16:23)* ... and *"whatever you ask in My name, that I will do, that the Father may be glorified in the Son..." (John 14:13).*

Our understanding of this comes from the fact that Jesus is the one and only "mediator" between us and God, whose redemptive work and shed blood has washed us of sin, making it possible to bring us before God's throne in faith with our requests. *"For there is one God and one Mediator between God and men, the Man Christ Jesus" (1 Timothy 2:5).* In other words, we have no sure access to God, except through Jesus Christ... thus we can only bring

70

our petitions before our Divine Creator, by means of our relationship to Jesus.

Does it matter which one we address our prayers to? Not really, as long as we come in the name of Jesus. Since all three members of the Godhead (trinity) are "one" ...that is God the Father, Jesus Christ the son, and the Holy Spirit... it would not seem improper to address any of the three in prayer. *"For there are three that bear witness in heaven: the Father, the Word, and the Holy Spirit; and these three are one" (1 John 5:7).*

However, scripture only provides examples of praying either to our Heavenly Father, or to the Lord Jesus. Such examples are seen as when Stephen was being stoned, he prayed to the Lord Jesus *(Acts 7:59)*, and when Paul exhorted the Ephesians to pray and give thanks to Father in the name of our Lord Jesus Christ *(Ephesians 5:20)*. There are no Biblical examples of praying directly to the Holy Spirit, but I have often welcomed His presence and expressed my thanksgiving to Him directly, for the many things He does in our lives.

21. Does it Help to Pray to Mary or the Saints?

There is no scripture to provide a basis for praying to Mary or any past saints or Apostles. Praying to a variety of revered personalities who have been deemed as "saints," is a "tradition" of the Catholic church, but is not found in the New Testament... thus not taught or followed by evangelical believers.

Mary, Jesus' earthly mother, was an exemplary follower of God, but neither she or any others can answer your prayers, or serve as a mediator in your behalf with God. Only Jesus can serve this purpose, *"For there is one God and one Mediator between God and men, the Man Christ Jesus"* *(1 Timothy 2:5).*

Faith in Jesus, and in the atoning work He performed for us on the cross, is the one and ONLY way that we can be saved and have access to God. Jesus said, *"I am the way, the truth, and the life. No one comes to the Father except through Me"* *(John 14:6).*

What about praying to "Allah?" Allah is an Arabic translation for God, most generally used by Muslims to refer to the God of their alleged prophet Muhammad. Christians do not, and must not, pray to the God of the Muslims.

Ironically, however, Arab Christians often refer to Allah as the Heavenly Father of Jesus Christ, to whom they've believed and surrendered their lives. Even though the same name, Allah, is sometimes used by both Arab Christians and Muslims, they don't refer to the same God. We can compare this to the name, Jesus *(Yeshua)*, God's son, that was also shared by others in Biblical times... and used in modern times as a popular first name in Hispanic culture. Thus, there many thousands who have shared the name, Jesus, but there's only one Jesus Christ, son of God.

Because a generic reference to God could be interpreted differently by persons of varying beliefs, Biblical personalities often identified their God as "the God of Abraham, Isaac, and Jacob" *(Acts 3:13).* Our Heavenly Father, of course, knows our heart, and understands to whom we're directing our prayers... which is further distinguished as we pray to Him in the name of His Son, Jesus.

22. Why Are Some Prayers Not Answered?

One of the greatest benefits afforded to every Christian is the privilege of answered prayers. In the Bible, Jesus made this tremendous promise, ***"And whatever things you ask in prayer, believing, you will receive" (Matthew 21:22).***

However, despite the Lord's willingness to answer prayer, it is obvious that some have gone unanswered. While the Bible can offer explanations for most instances, there are others that none of us can explain. I regret that sometimes there will be unanswered prayers that seem to have no reason, except only to conclude it simply wasn't the Lord's will for this present time. In such moments, don't falter or give up, but keep believing and trusting. God has a good plan in mind for each of us, which he will eventually reveal in His time. *"Trust in the Lord with all your heart, And lean not on your own understanding" (Proverbs 3:5).*

In the meantime, the following are some of the most common reasons why many prayers do not get results. In most cases, if we compare our heart and life against this checklist, we'll find the answer and be able to apply a Biblical solution.

(1) Lack of Fellowship with God and His word – *"If you abide in Me, and My words abide in you, you will ask what you desire, and it shall be done for you" (John 15:7).*

73

Unanswered prayers are sometimes a result of an absence of fellowship with the Lord and His Word. Jesus promised that if we would remain in His fellowship, and allow His Word to remain in us, this would produce results in prayer.

(2) Not Seeking to Please the Lord – *"And whatever we ask we receive from Him, because we keep His commandments and do those things that are pleasing in His sight" (1 John 3:22).* Answers to prayer come when we seek to keep His commandments and please the Lord with our life. This is not to suggest that we "earn" answered prayers, any more than we can earn salvation which comes only by faith *(Ephesians 2:8-9).* He answers our prayers from his "grace" and "mercy" *(Hebrews 4:16),* not merely from our good deeds. However, keeping His commandments and pleasing the Lord is a product of our obedience to His word, which is faith in action *(James 2:20).*

What are His commandments? He commanded that we are to love the Lord with all our heart, mind, and soul, and to love our neighbor as ourselves *(Mark 12:30-31).* Further, Jesus said we are to love our brethren as He has loved us. *"This is My commandment, that you love one another as I have loved you" (John 15:12).* Lack of love, bitterness, unforgiveness is the root of many unanswered prayers, since faith works by love *(Galatians 5:6).*

(3) Unconfessed Sin in One's Life – *"For the eyes of the LORD are on the righteous, And His ears are open to their prayers; But the face of the LORD is against those who do evil" (1 Peter 3:12).* There is no doubt that sin will disrupt the flow of God's blessings and answers to prayer. The psalmist, David wrote, *"If I regard iniquity in my* *heart, The Lord will not hear" (Psalms 66:18)*. All acts of rebellion and disobedience to God is considered sin. Sins of "commission," are those overt acts which are done in disobedience. However, sins of "omission," are those things we don't do in obedience, but know we should *(James 4:17)*. The remedy for all sin is to confess it to God, forsake it, and ask Him to forgive you *(1 John 1:9)*.

(4) Improper Motives – *"You ask and do not receive, because you ask amiss, that you may spend it on your pleasures" (James 4:3)*. Our motives in our prayer requests are important the Lord. He wishes to help us in our time of need, but is not obligated to answer prayers which will merely feed our carnal, worldly appetites and *(lustful)* pleasures. Our motives and desires can be corrected by humbling ourselves, and drawing near to God *(James 4:8-10)*.

(5) Not asking in God's will – *"Now this is the confidence that we have in Him, that if we ask anything according to His will, He hears us. And if we know that He hears us, whatever we ask, we know that we have the petitions that we have asked of Him" (1 John 5:14-15)*. God will only answer those prayers that are in "His" will. When we ask anything that is in His will, we can have assurance that those "petitions" (requests) are granted to us. God's will is revealed through His Word, the Bible. Anything promised by His Word is His will, and we can be confident that He'll honor our prayers based on His Word.

(6) Don't Know How to Pray – *"...Lord, teach us to pray..." (Luke 11:1)*. Some lack effectiveness in prayer simply because they don't know what the scriptures teach about prayer. Jesus gave His disciples an outline for prayer in Matthew 6:9-13. Take the time to study it. Other passages teach that prayer is primarily to be a private, intimate time with the Lord *(Matthew 6:6)*, to be intermingled with praise and thanksgiving *(Acts 16:25, Philippians 4:6)*. Times of fasting with prayer are beneficial to strengthen our faith and power in prayer *(Acts 14:23, 1 Corinthians 7:5)*. Jesus often went to secluded places to spend prolonged periods in prayer *(Luke 6:12, Matthew 4:2)*.

(7) Lack of Faith – *"But without faith it is impossible to please Him, for he who comes to God must believe that He is, and that He is a rewarder of those who diligently seek Him" (Hebrews 11:6)*. We cannot please God without faith. Prayer is not merely "begging" from God. It is "believing" God and His Word! Faith will come forth and grow as we devote our attention to the Word of God *(Romans 10:17)*. Our faith can also be "built up," by praying in the Holy Spirit *(Jude 1:20)*. In addition, prayer with fasting is often needed to help purge our faith from carnal, fleshly hindrances that can interfere with our prayers *(Matthew 17:20-21)*.

(8) Misunderstanding of Faith – *"Therefore I say to you, whatever things you ask when you pray, believe that you receive them, and you will have them" (Mark 11:24)*. Many do not understand that faith is believing in the reality of things, even though we cannot see them *(Hebrews 11:1)*. Jesus said that "when" you pray, you must believe that you "receive" your answer by faith. The word, "receive" comes from the Greek word, *lambanō (λαμβάνω)*, which means "to receive now" (present tense). He then says we will "have" them. "Have" comes from the word, *esomai (ἔσομαι)*, which means "to possess later" (future tense). So, when we pray we must believe in the finished results of our prayer... taking possession of the answer by faith, and we will eventually experience the tangible results sometime later.

The words of our mouth also play an important role to our faith as they tend to convey, and sometimes "betray," the contents of our heart. *"For out of the abundance of the heart his mouth speaks" (Luke 6:45).* The whole idea of receiving answers to prayer, is based on aligning our faith to believe and receive the promises declared in God's Word. In other words, if we really believe that God has heard our prayer, and that we have taken possession of His answer by faith, that should also be the testimony of our words.

No, I don't think we should be saying or telling others things like the "money is in the bank" when our account balance still shows zero... or that "the cancerous tumor is gone," even though it still appears in the x-rays. But rather, our words should express our faith in God's Word, instead of reflecting the discouraging doubt and despair of the problems still visible and obvious before us. I have often seen people rise from prayer with a sense of assurance that God has undertaken in their behalf, only to start chattering about their problems or symptoms, until their words pull them back down into a pit of despair and unbelief.

Prayer is a matter of coming into agreement with God's Word and promises... so let "His Word" be what you pray, believe and say concerning your needs or problems. Instead of blabbing discouragement about the empty bank account, apply God's Word to your heart, and to your words. Don't keep dwelling on or rehashing your problems, but keep focusing on God's promises. You can also pray something like, *"Lord Jesus, by faith, I receive your promise to meet my needs, and I stand on your Word, that 'my God shall supply all my need according to Your riches in glory by Christ Jesus'" (Philippians 4:19).* I personally always remind God of His many promises in my prayers, and quote chapter and verse from His Word, proclaiming my case of confidence in what He has said and will do.

Nonetheless, Jesus told us that our words were pretty important to God, so keep this mind as you pray and seek to embrace the promises of God. *"For by your words you will be justified, and by your words you will be condemned" (Matthew 12:37).*

(9) Wavering faith – *"But let him ask in faith, with no doubting, for he who doubts is like a wave of the sea driven and tossed by the wind. For let not that man suppose that he will receive anything from the Lord" (James 1:6-7).* There are those who allow every "wind" of circumstances to influence or discourage their faith. They vacillate back and forth, like the waves tossed about in the sea. One day they believe, but the next, they're ready to give up, and so forth. Such persons usually base their faith on their feelings or emotions instead of God's Word. They who waver in their faith cannot expect to receive "anything of the Lord." Our faith must become stable, steadfast, and consistent to receive from God.

(10) Failure to apply spiritual Authority – *"For assuredly, I say to you, whoever says to this mountain, Be removed and be cast into the sea, and does not doubt in his heart, but believes that those things he says will be done, he will have whatever he says" (Mark 11:23).*

There are times that some prayers may not get far until we declare the "spoken" authority of the name of Jesus and the Word of God. Among the reasons for this is that the problems we face may "sometimes" be a product of an evil spiritual origin. As Paul writes, *"For we do not wrestle against flesh and blood, but against principalities, against powers, against the rulers of the darkness of this age, against spiritual hosts of wickedness in the heavenly places" (Ephesians 6:12).* In such cases, our prayers may need to engage in "spiritual warfare" to obtain results.

The need for this type of prayer is especially obvious whenever Christians deal directly with demonic activity. For this evil operation to cease, our prayers need to include the exercise of spiritual authority against the devil in the name of Jesus, commanding him to leave *(Acts 16:18).* Therefore, as Jesus indicated, there are moments that we need to literally speak to mountains (symbolic of obstacles, problems or strongholds) and tell them to move in Jesus' name. Prayer with fasting, as we've previously mentioned, is often also needed to confront many of these types of challenges *(Matthew 17:20-21).*

(11) Lack of Perseverance - *"And let us not grow weary while doing good, for in due season we shall reap if we do not lose heart" (Galatians 6:9).* Probably the greatest reason that some prayers go unanswered is because many give-up praying and believing before they receive their answer. As long as we have the promise of God's Word, be patient and persistent. Keep believing, and don't quit, no matter how long it takes! God has a "due season" when He will bring the answer to pass.

79

23. How Often Should I Pray?

It goes without saying that Christians should pray every day, but the frequency or length of time spent in prayer is up to each individual as the Lord leads them. Prayer is an important part of your daily spiritual life... the very core of your relationship with God. Not only does the Lord desire such special moments of fellowship and conversation with you, He wants to impart His strength and encouragement that comes from spending time with Him.

The Jews had three established prayer times daily, as described by David, *"Evening and morning and at noon I will pray, and cry aloud, And He shall hear my voice" (Psalms 55:17)*. Although not mandated under the new law of Grace in the New Testament, this tradition was maintained by many early Christians. The psalmist also refers to other patterns that were practiced by some, such as *"Seven times a day I praise You, Because of Your righteous judgments" (Psalms 119:164)*.

The New Testament doesn't mention a specific prayer schedule as such, but rather suggests that prayer and fellowship with the Lord should be frequent and continual. This was what Paul was referring to, when he encouraged believers to *"pray without ceasing" (1 Thessalonians 5:17)*, and to *"continue steadfastly in prayer" (Romans 12:12)*.

Even though we can pray and converse with the Lord at the same time that we do other things, a prescribed time set aside to seek only the Lord, without other distractions, is still a good idea. *Corrie ten Boom once said, "Don't pray when you feel like it. Have an appointment with the Lord and keep it.*"[1] Something as simple as 15 minutes of prayer first thing in the morning might be a good place to begin. Perhaps you can expand that duration over time, or plan for other moments during your day.

Another good time to pray is when you sense an urging or nudging in your heart or spirit. This is usually the Holy Spirit prompting or inviting you to pray. While we may not always understand why, there are certain times or seasons that we are more sensitive to spiritual things... and moments that the Holy Spirit seems more accessible to us as well. When these opportunities emerge, seize the moment and call upon the Lord. *"Seek the Lord while He may be found, Call upon Him while He is near"* (Isaiah 55:6).

You will eventually discover that the time you spend with the Lord is well worth the investment... a necessary part of your spiritual strength and nourishment. *"But those who wait on the Lord Shall renew their strength; They shall mount up with wings like eagles, They shall run and not be weary, They shall walk and not faint"* (Isaiah 40:31).

[1] *The Hiding Place, Corrie Ten Boom, 1971*

24. If My Prayers Aren't Answered, Should I Give Up?

Absolutely not. As long as you know that your request is the will of God, persist in your faith and don't ever give up praying. And even if you're are unsure of His will, keep on praying until you have a grasp on what His plan is.

To illustrate the need for persistence in prayer, Jesus offered this parable about a widow who pestered a judge until he finally relented and brought justice to her dispute:

"One day Jesus told his disciples a story to show that they should always pray and never give up. There was a judge in a certain city, he said, who neither feared God nor cared about people. A widow of that city came to him repeatedly, saying, Give me justice in this dispute with my enemy. The judge ignored her for a while, but finally he said to himself, I don't fear God or care about people, but this woman is driving me crazy. I'm going to see that she gets justice, because she is wearing me out with her constant requests! Then the Lord said, Learn a lesson from this unjust judge. Even he rendered a just decision in the end. So don't you think God will surely give justice to his chosen people who cry out to him day and night? Will he keep putting them off? I tell you, he will grant justice to them quickly! But when the Son of Man returns, how many will he find on the earth who have faith?" (Luke 18:1-8 NLT).

As Jesus shared this story, He made an eye-opening comparison between the earthly judge and the Heavenly judge. He pointed out that if even a "secular judge," who has no special regard or favor for anyone, will eventually give-in to such persistence by the widow... how much more will God, the "righteous judge" of Heaven, eventually respond to your persistent prayers of faith? The obvious answer is that the Heavenly Father is far more eager to respond to your petitions than any secular magistrate.

Elsewhere, Jesus again addressed the issue of persistent prayer, but this time using the illustration of how a loving parent responds to the continual requests of their child. *"Keep on asking, and you will receive what you ask for.*

Keep on seeking, and you will find. Keep on knocking, and the door will be opened to you. For everyone who asks, receives. Everyone who seeks, finds. And to everyone who knocks, the door will be opened. 'You parents—if your children ask for a loaf of bread, do you give them a stone instead? Or if they ask for a fish, do you give them a snake? Of course not! So if you sinful people know how to give good gifts to your children, how much more will your heavenly Father give good gifts to those who ask him" (Matthew 7:7-11 NLT).

What is Jesus saying here? He is encouraging His followers to pray with the awareness that the Lord is loving and caring, "eager" to bless and answer their prayers, just as a dad wants to please his child. In fact, He suggests that if earthly parents are inclined to bless and do wonderful things for their kids, how much "more" will our Heavenly Father do even greater things for those who serve Him and pray. So, keep on Asking, keep on Seeking, keep on Knocking... don't give up, and you'll eventually get results.

George Mueller, the famed English missionary to orphans, whose miraculous prayers became legendary in the 19th century, said *"It is not enough to begin to pray, nor to pray aright; nor is it enough to continue for a time to pray; but we must patiently, believingly, continue in prayer until we obtain an answer."*[1]

In his diary, Mueller shared this example of his persistent prayers, unaware at the time, that the greatest illustration of his perseverance would come after his death.

*"In November 1844, I began to pray for the conversion of
five individuals. I prayed every day without a single
intermission, whether sick or in health, on the land, on the
sea, and whatever the pressure of my engagements might
be. Eighteen months elapsed before the first of the five was
converted. I thanked God and prayed on for the others.
Five years elapsed, and then the second was converted. I
thanked God for the second, and prayed on for the other
three. Day by day, I continued to pray for them, and six
years passed before the third was converted. I thanked God
for the three, and went on praying for the other two. These
two remained unconverted."[2]*

Thirty-six years later, Mueller noted again in his writings
that these two, sons of one of his friends, were still not
converted, but that he had continued praying for them.
*"But I hope in God, I pray on, and look for the answer.
They are not converted yet, but they will be."[2]* True to his
word, he continued praying for the men until his death in
1898. Finally, after Mueller passed away, more than fifty-
five years from when he first began, the answer to his
faithful prayers came... when both men were converted
and became followers of Christ.

[1] *George Müller of Bristol, Arthur Tappan Pierson, 1899*
[2] *George Müller: The Modern Apostle of Faith, By Frederick G. Warne,
1907*

25. Why Do Some Answers to Prayer Take so Long?

It would be terrific if we could receive answers to all our
prayers immediately, however we know it doesn't always
work that way. There can probably be a lot of reasons for
delays, some of which are known only to God... but it's

obvious that many things simply take time, and requires our determination and patience.

Sometimes our faith needs time to develop and grow in order to obtain the results we seek. This was the primary lesson behind Jesus' parable of faith as a mustard seed. When His disciples came to Him, seeking an explanation as to why their efforts to exorcise a demon had been unsuccessful, He used the tiny pin-head sized seed to illustrate the potential of what prayer and faith could do. *"Then the disciples came to Jesus privately and said, Why could we not cast it out? So Jesus said to them, Because of your unbelief; for assuredly, I say to you, if you have faith as a mustard seed, you will say to this mountain, Move from here to there, and it will move; and nothing will be impossible for you..." (Matthew 17:19-20).*

The point Jesus was making, was that the tiny mustard seed was not the final product... but if allowed time to grow and develop, just like our faith... it has the potential of sprouting to substantial size *(Luke 13:19)*. The strength of mustard seed faith lies with its patience and consistency. It may be subtle, almost invisible, like the tiny mustard seed... but as it remains steadfast, clinging to the soil... it grows patiently in small increments each day as it is watered and nurtured by God's Word. And eventually it's development will become evident, along with the desired impact of our prayers.

Answered prayers are also delayed because there is often a lot of activity and "spiritual warfare" in the unseen spiritual realm that we're sometimes aware of. For example, when Daniel received distressing visions about the future of his people, he prayed and sought the Lord for three weeks to understand their meaning, but received no answer to his prayers.

However, on the twenty-first day, Daniel was stunned by the unexpected appearance of an angelic visitor (likely a precarnate appearance of the Lord Jesus, compare Daniel 10:5-6 with Revelation 1:12-15) insomuch that he collapsed when he saw him and heard his voice.

Lifting him up from the ground, the visitor said, *"Daniel, you are very precious to God, so listen carefully to what I have to say to you. Stand up, for I have been sent to you. When he said this to me, I stood up, still trembling. Then he said, Don't be afraid, Daniel. Since the <u>first day</u> you began to pray for understanding and to humble yourself before your God, <u>your request has been heard in heaven</u>. I have come in answer to your prayer. But for twenty-one days the spirit prince of the kingdom of Persia blocked my way. Then Michael, one of the archangels, came to help me, and I left him there with the spirit prince of the kingdom of Persia. Now I am here to explain what will happen to your people in the future, for this vision concerns a time yet to come"* (Daniel 10:10-14 NLT).

Daniel must have been blown away to realize that God had heard his request from the first day he prayed... and to realize that his answer had been blocked by an agent of Satan, the spirit prince of Persia. But his many days of sustained prayers were necessary, to allow Michael and his angelic warriors to continue their assault against Satan's forces, so to bring Daniel the answer to his prayer.

"For the weapons of our warfare are not carnal but mighty in God for pulling down strongholds, casting down arguments and every high thing that exalts itself against

the knowledge of God, bringing every thought into captivity to the obedience of Christ" (2 Corinthians 10:4-5).

26. Does Fasting Provide a Beneficial Effect to Prayer?

Yes, absolutely! When combined with prayer and a sincere passion for God, fasting can have a powerful influence on the effectiveness of our prayer life as well as our spiritual relationship with the Lord. Prayer with fasting has been a long-established regimen of God's people, and was a standard practice of Jesus, His disciples and the early church. It is so important and vital for every believer, that it should be practiced on a regular, frequent basis.

Fasting is often thought of as simply abstaining from food, but it is much more than that. Its intent is to withdraw our attention from earthly and physical things, so to focus more clearly upon God and spiritual things. It is a type of discipline to humble our flesh, to reaffirm that we will not allow it or its desires, to manipulate or rule us... but that we give greater weight to our spiritual man in which God's presence dwells.

Before the New Testament, the Jewish people had a long history with fasting. Among other special days set aside for fasts, pious Jews observed weekly fast days of Mondays and Thursdays... which was what a certain hypocritical Pharisee was boasting about, when he said, *"I fast twice a week; I give tithes of all that I possess" (Luke 18:12).*

In the New Testament, Paul referred to prayer with fasting as something commonly practiced by believers *(1 Corinthians 7:5).* Jesus also expected His followers to fast, reminding them that *"when you fast,"* not to do so as a pious display, but as a private act of humility and sacred devotion to God *(Matthew 6:16-18)*.

There are also scriptures that associate fasting with prayer for special instances of God's presence or power, such as when hands were laid on Paul and Barnabas *(Acts 13:2-3)*, or to ordain and commission elders into ministry. *"So when they had appointed elders in every church, and prayed with fasting, they commended them to the Lord in whom they had believed" (Acts 14:23)*.

Scripture often associates fasting with seeking God passionately with one's "whole heart," such as by humbling ourselves before the Lord, repenting for sin, or seeking an answer or breakthrough from God. Such is illustrated when the prophet Joel called upon his people to repent for their sins. *"Now, therefore, says the Lord, Turn to Me with all your heart, With fasting, with weeping, and with mourning. So rend your heart, and not your garments; Return to the Lord your God, For He is gracious and merciful, Slow to anger, and of great kindness; And He relents from doing harm" (Joel 2:12-13)*.

Abstaining from food is meant to humble or "lower" our "self" nature before God, to bring our natural man under submission to Him, to decrease its impact over what we think, believe and do. One of many past leaders and scholars who wrote extensively about this was Derek Prince, who fasted at least one day a week during his entire adult life. Citing from many scripture passages, such as Isaiah 58:5-9, Prince taught that humbling self is really what the fasting is all about. He wrote that *"The primary purpose for fasting, as revealed in the Bible, is self-humbling. Fasting is a scriptural way to humble ourselves. All through the Bible God required His people to humble themselves before Him. God has revealed that a simple, practical way to humble ourselves is through fasting."*[1]

When combined together, prayer with fasting then becomes an intensified devotion toward God, drawing from His Spirit and strength... while also pulling away from earthly and physical influences and appetites. We might describe it as a discipline to tip the balance of what has leverage over us... away from our flesh nature, and toward the spiritual nature of God's presence. This internal conflict is something believers will always contend with, and we must "continually" humble and surrender ourselves to the Lord so that He and His presence will govern our thoughts, decisions and lifestyle, rather than the superficial sensual nature of our flesh.

This helps to understand why prayer with fasting has such a beneficial influence on the effectiveness of our faith. Unbelief draws its strength from the carnal influences of the flesh, which will challenge and interfere with the spiritual nature of faith. The flesh is also the target of Satan's many deceptions and temptations, through which he tries to disrupt or hinder our confidence in God and His Word. Consequently, prayer and fasting is a necessary ingredient to help purge the influences of unbelief, and to boost our sensitivity to the source of our faith, which is God and His Word.

An illustration of this can be seen in the instance when Christ's disciples were unsuccessful in their attempt to exorcise a demon from a man's son. In desperation, the man turned instead to Jesus for His help, who rebuked and expelled the devil. Later in private, the disciples came to Jesus, asking why they had failed. He replied that it was due to their unbelief... adding that this kind of challenge to their faith would require "prayer and fasting." *"Why could we not cast it out? So Jesus said to them, Because of your unbelief; for assuredly, I say to you, if you have faith as a mustard seed, you will say to this mountain, move from here to there, and it will move; and nothing will be impossible for you. However, this kind does not go out except by prayer and fasting"* (Matthew 17:19-21).

The famed Christian writer, Andrew Murray, once wrote, *"Prayer needs fasting for its full and perfect development... Prayer is reaching out after the unseen; fasting is letting go of all that is seen and temporal. Fasting helps express, deepen, confirm the resolution that we are ready to sacrifice anything, even ourselves to attain what we seek for the kingdom of God."*[2]

John Wesley believed so strongly in the spiritual importance of fasting that he refused to ordain young men to the ministry who would not fast two days each week.[3] Martin Luther fasted regularly, and so did John Knox. Charles Finney said, *"When empty of power I would set apart a day for private abstinence and prayer... after this, the power would return in all its freshness."*[4] Other legendary figures such as E.M Bounds, John Calvin, George Whitefield, Jonathan Edwards, Charles Spurgeon, D. L. Moody, Smith Wigglesworth, Oral Roberts, Gordon Lindsay, Lester Sumrall, Leonard Ravenhill, George Mueller, John Hyde and Billy Graham also were known to have made fasting, a part of their Christian discipline.

Finally, Bill Bright, the late founder of Campus Crusade for Christ, may have summed it up best from a single line in a little booklet he wrote. He said, *"Fasting is the most powerful spiritual discipline of all the Christian disciplines. Through fasting and prayer, the Holy Spirit can transform your life."*[5]

[1] *Fasting: The Key to Releasing God's Power in your Life, Derek Prince, 1993*
[2] *With Christ in the School of Prayer, Andrew Murray, 1898*
[3] *The spiritual discipline of fasting, Good News Magazine, Steve Johnson, 2012*
[4] *Power from on High, Charles Finney, 1874*
[5] *Your Personal Guide to Fasting and Prayer, Bill Bright, 1997*

27. What is a House of Prayer?

This term generally refers to an instance when Jesus rebuked money-changers and vendors who were selling sacrifices in the outer court of Herod's Temple in Jerusalem. Besides a violation of the Sabbath laws, Jesus considered this as an exploitation of the sacredness of God's house. Quoting from Isaiah 56:7, He scolded them, *"It is written, My house shall be called a house of prayer, but you have made it a den of thieves." (Matthew 21:13).*

The old covenant temple was specifically called a house of prayer, a place that was holy and sacred, where God interfaced with His people. However, technically speaking, this really cannot correspond to a church facility, because under the new covenant of Christ, the "believer" becomes God's temple. While every church building should be dedicated for prayer, God's people in today's era are the house or "household" of prayer... the tabernacle in whom the Holy Spirit dwells. *Do you not know that you are the temple of God and that the Spirit of God dwells in you?" (1 Corinthians 3:16).*

Prayer is indispensable to the Christian life and is the vital link to open the door to God's provisions, divine guidance, and solutions to every problem. Consequently, the body of Christ, the church, must be a people of prayer, dedicated to a life of spiritual devotion to God. For this reason, prayer should be one of the most important priorities of every church... not only encouraging everyone to pray individually, but also to facilitate opportunities of "corporate prayer," that is, believers gathering and praying together in agreement and harmony for the same requests, as the early church did *(Acts 2:42; 4:24; 20:36, 21:5).*

Such prayer meetings are not only inspiring and encouraging, but the Lord makes an extraordinary promise to those who gather in His name to pray. He pledges a special visitation of His presence "in the midst" of them... and assures that He will honor their prayers of agreement. Jesus said: *"I say to you that if two of you agree on earth concerning anything that they ask, it will be done for them by My Father in heaven. For where two or three are gathered together in My name, I am there in the midst of them" (Matthew 18:19-20).*

Such promises of the Lord are so spectacular, that the church should eagerly participate in this type of prayer frequently. And not only should corporate prayer be a part of every church service, but a congregation should also have specially designated prayer meetings... for Christ to manifest his presence in the midst of the body, and to answer their prayers of agreement. Such unified prayers mean that the Lord will respond, will take action, and will change many lives and situations that are brought before Him in faith and agreement.

Believers should gather to pray together for a lot of reasons... but none are more urgent and important than to pray for the ministry of their church. Such prayer and intercession can help assure the presence and anointing of God in the services... and bring down the strongholds of resistance, so souls will be more receptive to the Gospel and be saved. Praying for the pastors and leaders is also vital, so God's anointing will rest upon their lives and protect them from Satan's constant assaults and booby-traps. In addition, people who pray for the ministry of their church also become more sensitive to God's presence, enabling them to be more receptive toward the blessings He pours out on the overall body of believers.

While addressing the importance of church prayer meetings, Charles Spurgeon once said, *"I assert that the condition of a Church may be very accurately gauged by its Prayer Meetings. If the spirit of prayer is not with the people, the minister may preach like an angel, but he cannot expect success. If there is not the spirit of prayer in a Church there may be wealth, there may be talent, there may be a measure of effort, there may be an extensive machinery, but the Lord is not there. It is a sure evidence of the Presence of God that men pray as the rising of the thermometer is an evidence of the increase of the temperature."*[1]

Charles Finney also said that prayer meetings provide other residual spiritual benefits to the church, *"(1) to promote union, (2) to increase brotherly love, (3) to cultivate Christian confidence, (4) to promote their own growth in grace, (5) to cherish and advance spirituality, (7) to exercise the gifts of individual members of the church (8) to invite impenitent sinners, so the church may pray for them, (9) for sinners to come and receive prayer to become converted."[2]*

If your church conducts such prayer meetings, you should attend and participate. If it doesn't, it would be good to host your own. Invite other believers and friends to come together with you, perhaps in your home or elsewhere, so you and those gathered can experience Christ's remarkable blessings upon your prayers of agreement.

"Rejoice always, pray without ceasing, in everything give thanks; for this is the will of God in Christ Jesus for you" (1 Thessalonians. 5:16-18).

[1] *A Call to Worship, Charles Spurgeon, 1873*
[2] *Meetings for Prayer, Charles G. Finney, 1835*

28. What is "Effectual Fervent" Prayer?"

This is a phrase that originates in the King James version. *"The effectual fervent prayer of a righteous man availeth much" (James 5:16 KJV).* The two words, "effectual" and "fervent," are actually translated from a single Greek word, *energeo (ἐνεργέω)*, a cousin to our word for energy. Generally speaking, it conveys the idea of "energizing," similar to an electrical current that brings energy to a circuit. When applied to the passage, this suggests a type of prayer that is "passionate, heartfelt, heated, persistent" and so forth. The Amplified Bible, renders it another way that's especially illuminating: *"The earnest (heartfelt, continued) prayer of a righteous man makes tremendous power available [dynamic in its working]" (James 5:16 TAB).*

This kind of prayer is quite the opposite of a lethargic, repetitious or superficial type. And while passionate, it is not merely whipping up emotions, or generating exciting sounds or words... but expresses an intense sincere confidence in God. This might also be described as praying "radically," with everything you got, with all your heart... along the lines of what Jeremiah wrote, *"And you will seek Me and find Me, when you search for Me with all your heart" (Jeremiah 29:13).*

The late British Methodist minister, William Booth, also knew something about such radical prayer. In 1865, this 36-year-old Englishman founded the Salvation Army, with the intent to evangelize the poor, and literally changed his society with the Salvation message of Christ. He once said, *"You must pray with your might... That does not mean saying your prayers, or sitting gazing about in church or chapel, with eyes wide open, while someone else says them for you. It means fervent, effectual, untiring wrestling with God. It means that grappling with Omnipotence, that clinging to Him, following Him about, so to speak, day and night, as the widow did to the unjust judge, with agonizing pleadings and arguments and entreaties, until the answer comes and the end is gained."*

"This kind of prayer be sure the devil and the world and your own indolent, unbelieving nature will oppose. They will pour water on this flame. They will ply you with suggestions and difficulties. They will ask you how you can expect that the plans and purposes and feelings of God can be altered by your prayers. They will talk about impossibilities and predict failures; but, if you mean to succeed, you must shut your ears and eyes to all but what God has said, and hold Him to His own word: and you

*cannot do this in any sleepy mood; you cannot be a
prevailing Israel unless you wrestle as Jacob wrestled,
regardless of time aught else, save obtaining the blessing
sought—that is, you must pray with your might."[1]*

When I read such words by God's great men of the past, I
tremble at their passion and faith. Men such as Booth and
others stood on the front lines of intercession, and
persevered until God honored His fervent radical prayers
of faith.

In his book, The Essentials of Prayer, author E.M. Bounds
wrote, *"Prayer must be aflame. Its ardor must consume.
Prayer without fervor is as a sun without light or heat, or
as a flower without beauty or fragrance. A soul devoted to
God is a fervent soul, and prayer is the creature of that
flame. He only can truly pray who is all aglow for holiness,
for God, and for heaven."[2]*

As the scripture says, this type of *energeo* prayer, will
"avail much," or will have a prevailing effect, when
engaged by a "righteous person." And who is a righteous
person? Any believer who is washed in the blood of Jesus
Christ, forgiven of their sins, and who is walking after the
life and teaching of Jesus Christ.

Clearly, righteousness is not something that any of us can
attain by our actions alone. The Bible says that our own
efforts of righteousness are as worthless filthy rags
(Isaiah 64:6). However, when we place faith in Jesus, the
righteousness of Christ's Spirit comes to dwell within us,
elevating us to a status of righteousness in God's eyes
(who no longer sees our sins or blemishes), and this

generates a new nature of righteous behavior in the way we live and act.

In other words, righteous acts by themselves do not make us righteous in God's sight. Rather, a faith relationship with Christ is what brings about His righteousness ... and then the indwelling of His Holy (righteous) Spirit, produces the fruit of righteous behavior *(Galatians 5:9)*. *"Dear children, don't let anyone deceive you about this: When people do what is right, it shows that they are righteous, even as Christ is righteous" (1 John 3:7 NLT)*.

Interestingly, when the Holy Spirit inspired James to provide an illustration of such prayer, he chose Elijah, whose prayers God had used to demonstrate His mighty power. *"Elijah was a man with a nature like ours, and he prayed earnestly that it would not rain; and it did not rain on the land for three years and six months. And he prayed again, and the heaven gave rain, and the earth produced its fruit" (James 5:16-18)*

James' point was, that although Elijah's mighty prayers and exploits were legendary, he was also a man of frailties and flaws. This was never so obvious than when after being used to display God's power to Ahab, the wicked idolater and king of Israel, Elijah then recoiled in fear and fled from the threats of Jezebel, Ahab's wife. He actually crawled under a juniper tree where he asked the Lord to take his life *(1 Kings 19:2-4)*.

How can we make sense of such embarrassing behavior from this mighty man of God, whose prayers God used to control the weather for more than three years? This was the same man who called fire down from Heaven, and who destroyed four hundred and fifty prophets of Baal. The simple explanation is, Elijah was "human." He was a mere mortal, whose prayers God used in awesome and astonishing ways... but was still just an imperfect human being, just like you and me.

Thus, James message is clear. If God could hear and answer the passionate faith-filled prayers of Elijah, a common man "with a nature like ours," He can likewise hear and answer yours and mine. The Lord is eager to answer the effectual, fervent prayers of ordinary, but righteous followers of Jesus Christ!

[1] *God's Generals: The Revivalists, Roberts Liardon, 2008*
[2] *E. M. Bounds on Prayer, E. M. Bounds, 1922*

29. If God Already Knows My Needs, Why Pray?

It's true that God already knows your needs, as well as everything about your life *(Matthew 6:8)*. But because of limitations he's placed on Himself from interfering with man's free will, He needs for you to pray and invite His help to intervene in your life's affairs. This is in-part what Jesus meant when He told His followers that they should pray that the *"Father's will be done on earth, as it is in Heaven" (Luke 11:2)*.

The way God interacts with mankind is different than His other natural laws, which carry out His will and purposes regardless of man's choices. For instance, it's not necessary to pray for the earth to continue spinning on its axis, or to ask God to provide gravity, or air to breath. Long ago, God established these, and many other laws and patterns, which continue to function without our prayers or asking the Lord for assistance.

In addition, there are also many blessings that the Lord brings into the lives of His followers without them specifically asking. This is primarily because they've surrendered their lives to His will, and have already invited His participation in their lives by seeking to please Him and honor His principles *(Proverbs 16:7, Psalms 37:4, Matthew 6:33)*.

However, when faced with a need for God's intervention or assistance in the various problems or circumstances of life, we must pray in faith and ask Him for His help. As James wrote, *"you do not have because you do not ask" (James 4:2)*. When we pray, we can be assured that He is ready to hear and respond to the requests of His Children who call upon Him in Faith. Even as David wrote, *"Give ear, O Lord, to my prayer; And attend to the voice of my supplications. In the day of my trouble I will call upon You, For You will answer me" (Psalms 86:6-7)*.

The necessity of prayer is one of the most common themes of numerous Christian leaders down through the centuries, such as Charles Spurgeon, one of history's greatest preachers. He said *"Whether we like it or not, asking is the rule of the Kingdom. If you may have everything by asking in His Name, and nothing without asking, I beg you to see how absolutely vital prayer is."*[1]

Another more contemporary author and popular teacher on the subject of prayer, Stormie Omartian, also emphasized the need for prayer in her writings. In a book she co-authored with Jack Hayford, *The Power of Praying Together,* she wrote, *"Some people believe that God is going to do whatever He is going to do no matter what, so there is no reason to pray. But the truth is there are things God will not do on earth except in answer to prayer."²*

John Wesley, the famed founder of the Methodists, also taught and wrote much about the need for prayer. In his day, many failed to see prayer as a necessity, due to distorted teachings of predestination which misled people into thinking that their will was of no consequence. In their view, all events were predetermined and thus inevitable... so what would be the point of praying?

Such thinking is, of course, a twisted interpretation of Paul's teaching of God's prepared plan for those whom He "foreknows" *(Romans 8:28-29, Ephesians 1:5,11)*. This doesn't mean that man's fate has been predetermined against his will (a misguided belief known as fatalism). But rather, it simply means that God already "knows" the circumstances that man will face, the choices he will make... and has prepared a plan for Him accordingly. God also already knows the prayers you will pray, and is eager to bring His will and blessing into your life.

Wesley believed that God does nothing in man's affairs without prayer, and even went as far to argue that persons could not be converted to Christ without the prayers of someone, somewhere. He wrote, *"God does nothing but in answer to prayer; and even they who have been converted to God, without praying for it themselves (which is exceeding rare), were not without the prayers of others. Every new victory which a soul gains is the effect of a new prayer."³*

E.M. Bounds was another of history's great teachers and writers regarding prayer. He wrote, *"God has of his own motion placed himself under the law of prayer, and has obligated himself to answer the prayers of men. He has ordained prayer as a means whereby he will do things through men as they pray, which he would not otherwise do. If prayer puts God to work on earth, then, by the same token, prayerlessness rules God out of the world's affairs, and prevents him from working."[4]*

Consider something else. If prayer is necessary for God to intervene in our behalf, just imagine how many things have been attempted, even in His name for His purposes, without praying or seeking God. As amazing as this may sound, many churches actually attempt to do God's work without consulting Him or asking for His help. Sermons have been preached, classes taught, songs sung without seeking much if any of His guidance or blessing. So should it be a surprise if such attempts fail?

And even if some type of success is attained through man's efforts, what kind of true spiritual achievements can we hope to achieve for God, without His guidance or involvement? It reminds me of what Paul said about the temporal labors of man that will not endure *(1 Corinthians 3:15),* or those ministers who will appear before the Lord's Judgment, claiming many wonderful works they did in His name. Yet He will declare He never knew them *(Matthew 7:22-23).*

What we can conclude is, there's no assurance that God will intervene in the affairs of man apart from prayer. And without His intervention, we are helpless to save ourselves, or to overcome the wicked devices of Satan. Neither can we change our own lives, our circumstances, or our world in any lasting or meaningful way. As Jesus said, *"without Me you can do nothing"* (John 15:5).

Prayer is the means to acquire God's help, his blessings, and intervention... that He may manifest His will on the earth, as it is in Heaven. Without Him, we cannot accomplish anything lasting or meaningful. But with Him, we can achieve great things in His name, *"...with God all things are possible" (Matthew 19:26).*

Remember this, **"Without Him, you can do nothing... without prayer, He can do nothing."**

[1] *Ask and Have, Sermon Metropolitan Tabernacle, Newington London, C. H. Spurgeon, 1882*
[2] *The Power of Praying Together, Jack W. Hayford and Stormie Omartian, 2003*
[3] *A Plain Account of Christian Perfection, John Wesley, 1766*
[4] *The Weapon of Prayer, E.M. Bounds, 1922*

30. What Does It Mean to Pray Without Ceasing?

This idea comes mostly from Paul's admonition to the church of Thessalonica, to *"pray without ceasing" (1 Thessalonians 5:16-18).* He also made similar comments to the church at Rome, encouraging believers to keep on praying, just as he continued to do for them. *"Without ceasing I make mention of you always in my prayers" (Romans 1:9).* His thoughts were likely influenced by David's Psalm, who said *"In the day of my trouble I sought the Lord; My hand was stretched out in the night without ceasing..." (Psalms 77:2).*

Paul was not necessarily suggesting that persons are to pray at every given moment, but was emphasizing the importance of persistence and consistency. **Prayer is not a sprint, it's a marathon of faith, endurance and steadfastness.** His message was that prayer needs to continue on a frequent and ongoing basis, and without a disposition that it has been finished or concluded. Even when we receive answers to certain prayers, we only continue on praying for other persons or needs. And of course, our prayers, thanksgiving and worship are never ending as well.

While it was Jewish custom to pray three times during each day, *"Evening and morning and at noon" (Psalm 55:17, Daniel 6:10)*, prayer times for New Testament believers took on new dimensions of frequency. Spirit-filled Christians prayed more incessantly, about and for nearly everything, as the Spirit prompted them.

Although the New Testament doesn't promote particular times or frequencies for prayer, it goes without saying that we should be praying daily. But moreover, if we are following the leading of the Holy Spirit, we will likely be praying many times a day... for a variety of people, needs or situations that we come across.

It's been said that the famed evangelist, Smith Wigglesworth, would rarely pray more than fifteen minutes at a time, but also rarely went more than fifteen minutes without praying. Similar quotes have been attributed to Charles Spurgeon, as well as other notable men and women of God.

Prayer without ceasing also implies a perpetual search for things to pray for. Even when nothing seems obvious or urgent, there are so many matters we should always be praying for... such as our family, our nation, our church. For instance, Samuel considered it a sin not to pray for his people *(1 Samuel 12:23)*, and Paul wrote that we should always be praying for fellow believers in Christ. He said,

"...Stay alert and be persistent in your prayers for all believers everywhere" (Ephesians 6:18 NLT).

When Jesus told us to pray for the Father's *"will be done on earth as it is in heaven" (Matthew 6:10)*, He did so for a good reason. Because unless we pray and ask, He limits Himself from intervening in man's earthly affairs. As John Wesley said, *"God does nothing but by prayer, and everything with it."*[1]

Everyone should have a prayer list of people and issues to pray for. And among other things, we should also continually pray for our own heart to be humbled before the Lord, asking Him for a greater hunger and passion for matters that are important to Him.

"And let us not grow weary while doing good, for in due season we shall reap if we do not lose heart" (Galatians 6:9).

[1] *A Plain Account of Christian Perfection, John Wesley, 1766*

31. What is the Prayer of Faith?

There's only one specific reference to "prayer of faith" in the Bible. It comes from this passage in James, *"the prayer of faith will save the sick, and the Lord will raise him up..." (James 5:15)*. This prayer of faith for the sick will incorporate obedience to God's Word by calling on elders of the church, anointing the sick persons with oil, (a symbol of the Holy Spirit), and praying for these with faith in the Lord Jesus and His Word *(James 5:14)*.

Praying in faith means to pray authoritatively in the name of Jesus, laying claim to what God's Word says and promises about healing... with confidence that God will honor His Word and make persons well. Such prayers may also include spoken commands, such as when Peter prayed for the lame man at the temple gate. He declared, *"In the name of Jesus Christ of Nazareth, rise up and walk" (Acts 3:6).* Peter then took him by the hand, and the man's feet received strength... and not only did he walk, but also leaped while praising God.

However, praying in faith is not confined only for those who are sick... but is necessary for any prayers to be effective. Praying in faith means to believe that He will hear us when we seek Him, and will also respond by bringing answers to our requests in accordance to the promises of His Word. Notice from this passage how important your faith is to God, *"But without faith it is impossible to please Him, for he who comes to God must believe that He is, and that He is a rewarder of those who diligently seek Him" (Hebrews 11:6).*

Because of God's vast power, mercy and grace, it's a startling thing to see the word "impossible," used in relation to Him in any way, but this is the unfortunate result of unbelief. Faith is such an important issue to God, it's not possible to attain His favor without it. One's multitude of words or eloquence of prayer expressions, cannot overcome this. The only thing that impresses God about our prayers... is faith.

Since God is omnipotent (all powerful), it would be incorrect to suggest that anything can impose limitations on Him. However, He has "chosen" to limit Himself to the boundaries of faith for reasons of His own. In fact, you may recall the many stories of Jesus going about healing and performing great miracles, until He returned to minister in His own hometown. To the residents of

Nazareth, Jesus was just another common kid who grew up there, the son of a local carpenter. So how could he now be viewed as God's Son sent from Heaven to heal the sick and forgive sins? Scripture says that, *"He did not do many mighty works there because of their unbelief"* *(Matthew 13:58).*

32. What is Faith?

Faith is something often misunderstood because of so many ways the term is used by the secular world... sometimes to convey a wish or hope, or perhaps an optimism or belief in a person or thing.

Vine's Expository Dictionary of New Testament Words says that "faith" comes from the Greek, *"pistis"* (πίστις) which means a *"firm persuasion."* However, the Epistle to the Hebrews, provides a more elaborate description. It says, *"Faith is the substance of things hoped for, the evidence of things not seen"* *(Hebrews 11:1).*

I can recall the first time I took an in-depth look at this passage, only to be surprised when I realized it wasn't referring to something vague or ethereal as I originally thought about faith. The words "substance" and "unseen evidence," are absolute terms that describe things that exist, although not visible.

"Substance" is an interesting choice of words to describe faith. It essentially means something that's "real" or "tangible." However, we find something even more intriguing from its original Greek root, *hupostasis* (ὑπόστασις), which is derived from two other words. It comes from *"hupo,"* that means "beneath," along with *"histemi,"* something that "stands or supports." When

106

combined, *hupostatis* conveys the idea of "something real that stands under," very similar to the foundation of a house... though obscured from view, serves as the underlying framework on which the structure rests.

I think the Holy Spirit inspired the original word *hupostasis*, not only to express the substance and "certainty" of things hoped for (*"elpis" Ἐλπίς*), something we anticipate that has not yet occurred), but also to emphasize that faith is actually what "stands beneath," and serves as the infrastructure of those things.

This idea seems confirmed by scripture, as we read on to the third verse: *"By faith we understand that the worlds were framed by the word of God, so that the things which are seen were not made of things which are visible"* (Hebrews 11:3). Note the reference to invisible things as the framework for visible things, just as stated similarly about faith in verse 1. When we compare verses 1 and 3, we can see that both "Faith" and "God Word" share the same kind of unseen characteristics that also provide a framework for physical tangible things.

Faith and God's Word are so closely intertwined because they are essentially one in the same. Faith "is" God's Word, as it is believed and applied through the life of a Christian. The Bible says that faith comes by hearing God's Word *(Romans 10:17)*, so when a person opens their heart to receive His Word... faith becomes activated, which will bring the assurance of things not yet seen... *"the substance of things hoped for, the evidence of things not seen."*

Faith is something that the Holy Spirit imparts to the Lord's followers, so they can perceive spiritual things, and believe in His Word the way He does. Another way to put it, faith enables us to know what God knows, to see what He sees. The natural state of man's senses can't comprehend or believe in unseen realities. But faith overshadows such limitations, enabling us to perceive and believe in things that are impossible and unimaginable to human flesh. *"Eye has not seen, nor ear heard, Nor have entered into the heart of man The things which God has prepared for those who love Him... But God has revealed them to us through His Spirit" (1 Corinthians 2:9-10).*

God doesn't see limitations or impossibilities in connection to His Word, thus faith allows us to perceive His promises like He does... fulfilled and accomplished, "before" they become material or physical realities. Scripture says that God *"calls those things which do not exist as though they did" (Romans 4:17).* He is the Almighty Creator whose Words have creative ability, that no force or obstacle can resist. He merely says *"let there be light,"* and light appears. Further, He says, *"So shall My word be that goes forth from My mouth; It shall not return to Me void, But it shall accomplish what I please, And it shall prosper in the thing for which I sent it" (Isaiah 55:11).*

Faith, therefore, is not merely a matter of positive thinking, nor pretending that something is real when it's not... or a number of other wacky ideas that seem to float around. Rather, faith is a deep spiritual certainty, based on the real but unseen substance of God's Word. It's essentially a revelation that comes to us from the Holy Spirit that affirms the spiritual reality of things not seen to the natural eye... assuring us that we have taken "possession" of whatever He has promised. Faith enables us to see our prayer petition as something God has granted and fulfilled, and only awaits the appropriate time to be revealed.

This was what John was referring to when he said, *"And if we know that He hears us, whatever we ask, we know that we <u>have</u> the petitions that we have asked of Him" (1 John 5:15).* Faith enables us to receive the present-tense possession of the answer, before we ever see any tangible evidence of it, as Jesus described, *"whatever things you ask when you pray, believe that you <u>receive</u> them, and you will have them" (Mark 11:24).*

33. How Do I Acquire Faith?

The short answer is found from this verse, *"faith comes by hearing, and hearing by the word of God" (Romans 10:17).* As my pastor said many times when I was a young believer, *"Just open your heart to the Word of God and believe it."* Of course, the "hearing" referred to was not merely listening with one's natural ears, but opening one's heart to the scriptures, and allowing them to speak to our inner man.

If it sounds simple, it's because it is... insomuch that even a child can believe and exercise remarkable faith *(Matthew 18:3).* However, it's not always been so easy for everyone to understand, especially those who've not grown up with some exposure to belief in God or the Bible.

What I've found is, that if anyone will give God's Word a chance to bear witness of itself, and will allow for a bit of patience and persistence, it will eventually speak to even the most agnostic hearts and minds, such as seen in this example some years ago.

I was asked to make a pastoral visit to an older gentleman in the hospital who was seriously ill. His wife was a church member, quite firm in her faith, but her husband had never received Christ and she was fearful he would slip into eternity without being saved.

I had never met Lloyd before, but when I arrived he seemed respectful and listened to what I had to say. I shared scripture, prayed, and encouraged him to simply believe in Jesus Christ, to accept His forgiveness and promise of salvation. However, at this, he admitted his skepticism... finding it inconceivable to believe in spiritual things he couldn't see, touch or prove. *"I would really like to believe,"* he admitted, *"but I can't, I don't know how!"*

I explained as much as I could about the authenticity of Jesus and the Gospels, and we discussed what it meant to have faith... but it was obvious that his intellect was not convinced. Even if shown indisputable proofs, it still all boiled down to a matter of whether he was able or willing to believe it from his heart.

Tangible evidence that supports the validity of Jesus and the Gospel is important and essential, however faith is much more than mere head-knowledge of facts. Instead, it deals with matters of evidence that cannot be detected with the natural senses. Faith is a revelation of truth conveyed to one's open heart, by the Spirit of God's Word.

If proofs "alone" could produce faith, the many thousands who saw Jesus face-to-face, who witnessed His earthly ministry, teachings and miracles... would all have believed. But clearly, not everyone did... in fact, far more rejected Jesus and His teachings than received him.

While I was disappointed that Lloyd didn't respond immediately and believe on Jesus, but I was encouraged by his honest and humble reply, that he "wanted to believe!" This reminded me of the father who brought his demonized son to Jesus for help, but also struggled with his faith. *"Lord, I believe... but help my unbelief!" (Mark 9:24).* His humble confession and appeal for the Lord's assistance wasn't a setback, but in fact served to his benefit, in that Jesus responded favorably to his humility, strengthened his faith and delivered the child.

In my view, Lloyd's sincerity and desire to believe was something similar. It's a fact that God can work with any person who genuinely "wants" to believe, who is "willing" to open their heart to His truth. All God needs is a willingness to believe as much as we know how... and the seed of His Word will quickly blossom in such fertile soil. It's the nature of the God's Word to bear witness of itself, which will come alive and bring a surge of faith to any heart that will become open to receive it.

I encouraged Lloyd to reach out to the Lord, to open the Bible and let God's Word speak to His heart... which is what eventually what he did. He survived his health crisis, and began to come and listen to the Bible messages I preached, reviewing the scriptures for himself. And as he pondered God's Word, something inexplicable about its message overcame his intellectual reservations, and showed him how to believe in things he couldn't see, touch or prove. Faith came alive in his heart, and He believed upon Jesus and the truth of the Gospel.

The Bible is unlike any other book in the world. It is a spiritual text designed to communicate God's Words to the hearts of men and bring faith. While the printed pages appear like any other book, providing marvelous facts, history and details that speak to man's intellect... it also conveys spiritual truth that can only be perceived spiritually, from hearts that are open to His spiritual wavelength. This spiritual content is in-part what Jesus was referring to when he said, *"The words that I speak to you are spirit, and they are life" (John 6:63).*

This is the same basis for what Jesus inferred when he asked Peter if he understood His true identity. When Peter replied, *"You are the Christ, the Son of the Living God,"* Jesus affirmed that such awareness did not emerge solely from human knowledge or secular evidence. He explained that it came to Peter by revelation of God's Spirit. *"Blessed are you, Simon Bar-Jonah, for flesh and blood has not revealed this to you, but My Father who is in heaven" (Matthew 16:17).*

What happened with Lloyd, is the same thing that occurred with me decades ago when I first began to ponder the scriptures from an open heart... and which has been repeated by millions over the centuries. The Holy Spirit "illuminates" or "quickens"[1] the scriptures of God's Word *(logos, λόγος)*, so that they become alive as God's uttered Word *(rhema, ῥῆμα)*, or as though He is speaking to us in real time. This is how faith is supposed to originate... it comes by hearing God speak to our heart *(Romans 10:17).*

What I often find disheartening, however, are some who preach the message of the Bible, which is designed to bring faith... yet they warn hearers to avoid building up "false expectations" for miracles or answers to prayer. The fact is, if ministers of the Gospel will simply deliver the "untainted" message of God's Word without their faithless commentaries, His Word will bear witness of its truth, and will do everything God designed for it to do... to bring faith, and answered prayers!

¹ An old KJV term that means to "make alive."

34. Where Does Faith Come From?

Simply stated, Faith is something that comes from God. That is, He's the one who enables you to believe in Himself... just as He's the one who devised the plan for man's redemption from his fall in the Garden of Eden. He is also the one who sent Jesus (God, Himself, in the flesh) to suffer and die on the cross as the substitute for your sins, and the same one who provided Salvation to you as a free gift. And, likewise, He's the one who draws you to Himself, as Jesus said, *"No one can come to Me unless the Father who sent Me draws him" (John 6:44).*

Understanding the source of faith is important, so we know where to turn to strengthen and grow our faith. This will also help us avoid the error of trying to fabricate faith by our own fleshly works, which is both a stumbling block to our relationship with Christ, as well as receiving answers to prayer.

We may recall that James said that *"faith without works is dead" (James 2:26),* a reminder that believers are charged to act upon what they believe. How important it is to add action to our faith, to obey and follow the Lord in word and deed. But we cannot generate faith from self-works, any more than we can save ourselves through our own efforts. Faith is something that God transmits to you through His Word and Spirit... which then moves upon you to apply and exercise, as if a conduit through which He and His Word can flow.

Wherever faith is discussed in scripture, it always points back to God's divine source:

(1) Faith Comes by Hearing God's Word.
"So then faith comes by hearing, and hearing by the word of God" (Romans 10:17).

(2) Jesus is the Author (originator) and Finisher of our Faith.
"looking unto Jesus, the author and finisher of our faith..." (Hebrews 12:2)

(3) Saving Faith is a Gift that Comes from God.
For by grace you have been saved through faith, and that not of yourselves; it is the gift of God," (Ephesians 2:8).

(4) God Gives a Measure of Faith to Every "Believer."
"For I say, through the grace given to me, to everyone who is among you, not to think of himself more highly than he ought to think, but to think soberly, as God has dealt to each one a measure of faith" (Romans 12:3).

(5) The Spiritual Gift of Faith.
"to another faith by the same Spirit..." (1 Corinthians 12:9)

(6) Jesus said to have "God's faith."
Christ's admonition to *"Have faith in God" (Mark 11:22),* comes from the Greek, *ecete pistin qeou,* which seems to more literally say *"Have faith of God"* ...or as *The Bible in Basic English*[1] puts it, *"Have God's*

114

faith." (Perhaps such mountain-moving faith refers to a special gift, as Paul suggests in 1 Corinthians 13:2.)

(7) Faith as a Fruit of the Spirit (or faithfulness). *"But the fruit of the Spirit is love, joy, peace, longsuffering, gentleness, goodness, faith" (Galatians 5:22 KJV)*

(8) Faith Strengthened and Built Up by Praying in the Holy Spirit.
"But you, beloved, building yourselves up on your most holy faith, praying in the Holy Spirit." (Jude 1:20)

Realizing faith's source also helps remind us that **faith is a "spiritual" thing,** a product of your relationship with God, something important to remember in your walk with the Lord.

Faith isn't only a matter of doing, saying or praying the right things... it's being connected to God through His presence and Holy Word... and we must always be on guard lest we find ourselves drifting toward a disposition that tries to engage spiritual things from fleshly means.

It can happen very easily to any of us, if we don't sustain ourselves through prayer and His Word. Our heart will grow cold and distant from intimacy with God. Even though we may continue on with familiar religious routines, they will become lifeless repetitious patterns, instead of expressions of faith, joy and passion from God's presence. Faith involves works and actions, but these alone can never take the place of the spirit of faith that God places in your heart *(2 Corinthians 4:13)*, from which your acts of faith and devotion will flow.

If or whenever we find ourselves just going through the

motion of lifeless religious deeds, we need to break out of that empty form, and get back to the source of our spiritual life... Jesus. By opening His Word and seeking His presence through prayer, He will again revive the freshness of His presence and renew our faith and spiritual passion.

[1] *The Bible in Basic English, Cambridge Press, England, 1965*

35. Do Our Spoken Words Affect Our Faith?

Yes, but let's first look at a variety of passages that illustrate the importance that God puts on "all" our words and the things we say.

Jesus explained that what we express with our mouth, conveys the kinds of things that fill our heart. *"For out of the abundance of the heart the mouth speaks," (Matthew 12:34).* Just as a tree will produce fruit that reflects its nature, the things a person says from their mouth, will ultimately expose the true contents of their heart *(Matthew 12:35).*

And to leave no doubt as to how serious the Lord views our words, He made this amazing declaration about the accountability that will be required of all the things we say. He said, *"...for every idle word men may speak, they will give account of it in the day of judgment. For by your words you will be justified, and by your words you will be condemned," (Matthew 12:36-37).*

Even our casual expressions or frivolous comments will be called into review on the Day of Judgment... something that should give us pause, to think carefully before we utter anything. To realize that God is listening and

116

keeping a record of our words, should make us rethink our willingness to use filthy profanity, to say hateful or hurtful things, or to pass along unfounded rumors or gossip. Paul said, *"Let no corrupt word proceed out of your mouth, but what is good for necessary edification, that it may impart grace to the hearers" (Ephesians 4:29).*

In particular, however, Jesus was referring to things expressed from our heart, that can either justify or condemn us... that either profess faith in the Lord Jesus, or that deny Him and His forgiveness. Such words can literally determine our fate, as the scripture says, *"Death and life are in the power of the tongue..." (Proverbs 18:21).*

The Apostle Paul also helped us understand the essential relationship of one's tongue to what they believe. While pointing out that belief is an internal process of the heart, he explained that an outward confession of that belief was also necessary, to establish one's saving faith. Early believers often expressed this together with being baptized in water, as their first public acknowledgment of their new faith in Jesus. He said, *"If you confess with your mouth the Lord Jesus and believe in your heart that God has raised Him from the dead, you will be saved. For with the heart one believes unto righteousness, and with the mouth confession is made unto salvation" (Romans 10:9-10).*

Prior to Paul's epistle, Jesus had already addressed the matter of confessing Him publicly. He stated that it was a non-negotiable requirement for all believers, without which He would not confess them before the Heavenly Father. And though similar to Paul's remarks, His seemed to suggest an "ongoing" public confession, as might be expressed to friends, family, or perhaps public meetings.

"Therefore whoever confesses Me before men, him I will also confess before My Father who is in heaven. But whoever denies Me before men, him I will also deny before My Father who is in heaven" (Matthew 10:32-33).

James also had a lot to say about the use of the tongue, but especially how it can be misused to spew poison and cause harm, not only to others, but also to ourselves *(James 3:1-12).* He explained that the things we say, tend to exert a great deal of influence over the patterns of our life, very similar to a ship's rudder, or the bridle of a horse, used to steer its direction *(James 3:3-4).*

While he conceded that believers will continue to contend with a variety of human flaws, those who grow and become mature in the Lord, are ones whose tongues become more disciplined from its unruly sinful nature. *"If anyone does not stumble in word, he is a perfect [mature] man, able also to bridle the whole body" (James 3:1).*

Taming the wild impulsive nature of our tongue, however, is not something any of us can do on our own *(James 3:8),* but can only be accomplished by yielding ourselves to the indwelling power of His Holy Spirit *(Galatians 5:19-24).*

Meanwhile, among the more positive uses of our tongue, offering expressions of praise, worship and thanksgiving to God, is among of the most delightful and beneficial. *"Therefore by Him let us continually offer the sacrifice of praise to God, that is, the fruit of our lips, giving thanks to His name" (Hebrews 13:15)*

The psalmist says that we should tell of the Lord's wonderful redemption in our lives, *"Let the redeemed of the Lord say so..." (Psalms 107:2),* and to celebrate the greatness and wonders of the Lord with singing and rejoicing. *"Shout joyfully to the Lord, all the earth; Break forth in song, rejoice, and sing praises" (Psalms 98:4).*

Such jubilance not only pleases the Lord, but since He "inhabits" or dwells in the presence of such worship *(Psalm 22:3),* He also blesses and ministers to those who praise and worship Him. Such as what He did for Paul and Silas who prayed and sang praises in their prison cell throughout the night hours. As are result, God sent an earthquake that literally shook the foundations, loosed them from their chains, and burst open the doors *(Acts 16:24-26).*

Faith Has Something to Say

So, what we see from these and other passages, is that what we say is so significant to God... that our words can literally determine our life or death, justification or condemnation. Jesus stated clearly that He will not claim anyone who does not confess Him publicly, and Paul wrote that while believing in Christ is something that must occur within one's heart, it must also be confessed outwardly with our mouth.

Consequently, the things we say are also important to our relationship with prayer and faith. If we accept what Jesus said about the correlation between our heart and words *(Matthew 12:34),* it means that our tongue will reflect the kind of things that fill our heart.

In other words, if our heart is full of faith and God's Word... which it must to be effective in prayer, such things will be expressed from things we say. In fact, since scripture teaches us to act upon our faith with works *(James 2:17-22),* our words may often serve as the first works... or the initial, physical evidence of what we believe

119

(to be also followed with lifestyle changes that reflect our faith).

Paul seemed to infer something similar as the motivation behind his words and preaching... suggesting, in fact, that this is the nature of faith. When faith comes alive in our heart and spirit, it has something that wants to be said. *"And since we have the same spirit of faith, according to what is written, I believed and therefore I spoke, we also believe and therefore speak" (2 Corinthians 4:13).*

Faith is something spiritual, unseen, that's birthed inside us... but is implemented through outward words and actions. As Paul explained, saving faith begins by believing on the Lord Jesus in one's heart... but must also be confessed with the mouth to become effective (*Romans 10:9-10*). Why should faith be applied any differently for the other benefits of His atonement, or promises from God's Word?

So what does it means to confess the Lord Jesus? The Greek root for "confess" is *homologeó (ὁμολογέω)*, which means to "say the same thing." Faith believes and says the same things as God's Word. In this case, Paul explains that we are to agree with or say the same thing that the Gospel says about Jesus. ***"If you confess with your mouth that <u>Jesus is Lord</u> and believe in your heart that God raised him from the dead, you will be saved" (Romans 10:9 NLT).***

This, of course, will be stated in a personal way, something like, *"Jesus is now my Lord!"* (And since Lord means "master," this will also mean surrendering your life to follow Him and His teachings, as your new "boss.")

But what if we're praying and asking the Lord about other matters... such as meeting our needs, or perhaps healing of sickness? As we've already stated, **Faith always believes and says what God's Word says.**

Until answers to prayers come, it's so easy to become occupied with the problems, to complain about the pain, the difficulties, the circumstances. However, instead, it's so important to keep your heart and thoughts filled with God's Word and prayer, that builds and strengthens your faith. Instead of focusing or talking about the problems, fill your mouth with His Word, saying and quoting His promises aloud, remain focused on what He has said. Praise Him and thank Him for the promises of His Word, for hearing your prayers, and for the solutions He is working out behind the scenes.

Whenever I pray for anything, I first always want to be sure that I'm basing my requests on His will, which is declared from His Word. Thus, I go to the scriptures and lay out my petitions from the promises He has declared, reminding Him of these as I pray and seek His help. And after I pray and request His help, I continue expressing my praise and thanksgiving... and keep on believing, praying and saying what His Word says, claiming and declaring His promises to me.

Answers to prayers do not always come immediately, and often require patience and persistence. But fortunately, there's thousands of fantastic faith-building promises to review and keep our attention in the Bible during those delays.

For instance, pertaining to healing, there are scores of great promises (many which I quote elsewhere in this writing), but here's one of my favorites that I have frequently quoted and prayed, from a Psalm of David. *"Bless the Lord, O my soul, And forget not all His benefits: Who forgives all your iniquities, Who heals all your diseases" (Psalms 103:2-3).* Isn't this fantastic? Don't forget ALL the benefits that the Lord has to offer. Not only will He forgive and cleanse you of all your sins, but He can also heal all your diseases!

During times I've been seriously ill, I've often claimed and recited this and other similar promises, while praying, meditating, or as I sing praises and thanksgiving to God. Worshiping the Lord with devotion and gratitude is an especially wonderful expression of faith, which He honors and blesses in many ways. *"Whoever offers praise glorifies Me; And to him who orders his conduct aright I will show the salvation of God" (Psalms 50:23).*

God has answered my prayers and brought healing many times, but I'll never forget one especially scary challenge to my health many years ago. It was the same year my wife became expectant with our daughter, just prior to accepting our first pastorate. It started as what seemed to be an occasional throbbing pain on the left side of my head, but grew more intense and constant behind my left eye over a period of weeks.

I was a young itinerant evangelist in those days, didn't have insurance and rarely visited the doctor, but my symptoms became so serious that I eventually went. After doing a few tests and ruling out minor issues, he couldn't conclude a diagnosis without more analysis, but offered a few alarming possibilities. Needless to say, I was shocked when he said it could possibility be cancer or a brain tumor. I didn't know what to tell my wife, or where to get money for more tests or needed treatments. But after pondering and praying, I made a fateful decision... to go it alone without the doctor. It was frightening, but felt I had no choice but to put my faith in the Lord, and trust my life in His hands.

However, my fears were soon diminished by many faith-building scriptures I came across, especially this one that I'd never seen before: *"It is better to trust in the Lord Than to put confidence in man" (Psalms 118:8)*. This passage really blew me away, as I realized I wasn't the first one to stake his life on faith in God! And He apparently brought the writer of the passage, David, through his troubles pretty well!

Prayer and God's Word was already a big part of my life, but became more intense as I fasted, prayed and quoted God's healing promises day and night. However, the pain became so intense at times, discouragement would set in... and all I could think about was dying, leaving my wife and unborn baby behind.

It was then I really learned to fight the fight of faith, to resist such faith destroying attacks of depression and discouragement. I would march around the house, rebuking the devil, stomping my feet, praying, singing and shouting God's promises, until my joy and confidence in God's promises resurged. I even got large poster boards, and used markers to copy healing scriptures, which I taped on the walls throughout our house. So everywhere I looked, I saw God's promises, and would pray and meditate on them around the clock.

This sort of thing went on for the most part of a year, but as weeks passed I noticed a gradual decline of the pain and symptoms. It was still there, and could sometimes be intense, but I felt like God was answering my prayers.

Coincidentally, answers to other prayers also began emerging, such as our search for God's direction. My wife and I didn't think it feasible to continue traveling with a new baby... but before we could even compose a resume or look for a position, out of the blue, a church called and asked us to come and be their pastor!

So, after suffering this ailment for eleven months, I finally felt the last twinges of pain leave! It was during the first few weeks of our new pastorate, and just a couple months before the birth of our sweet baby girl. That was thirty-seven years ago, and the symptoms never returned. Praise the Lord!

I've not shared this to suggest that anyone should avoid physicians or medical treatment. Back at that time, I had no health coverage and felt I had no choice. But God used this experience to teach me that He is trustworthy with my life, and that I can depend on Him for anything. I'm grateful that today I have wonderful Christian physician, who even prays for me as well as administering medical assistance.

However, the message I do want to get across is that you can definitely trust God with your health and life. Even though we should value the advice and treatment offered by our physician, no one should ever put faith in man. Even my Christian doctor has to trust God to give him guidance in helping his patients. Put your faith in God, who will never fail you.

36. Are We Really Supposed to Speak to Mountains?

The idea of talking to mountains and relocating them, sounds pretty far-fetched. But considering that it was mentioned three times in two Gospels *(Matthew 17:20, 21:21, Mark 11:23)*, and even referred to by Paul *(1 Corinthians 13:2)*, it's obviously something important that Jesus wanted us to understand about faith.

In the instance from Mark's Gospel, Jesus and his disciples were returning to Jerusalem from Bethany, when Peter noticed a withered fig tree they had passed the day before. He was astonished that it had already shriveled and died, just since Jesus cursed it the day before (after finding it fruitless). In response to Peter's reaction, Jesus used the opportunity to offer more teaching to His disciples about prayer and faith.

Jesus said, *"Have faith in God. For assuredly, I say to you, whoever says to this mountain, 'Be removed and be cast into the sea,' and does not doubt in his heart, but believes that those things he says will be done, he will have whatever he says. Therefore I say to you, whatever things you ask when you pray, believe that you receive them, and you will have them"* (Mark 11:22-24).

First, while His admonition began by saying, *"Have faith in God,"* most English translations seem to shade its meaning slightly from the original. The phrase, *ecete pistin qeou (ἔχω πίστις θεός)*, appears to more literally say *"Have faith of God"* ...or as *The Bible in Basic English* puts it, *"Have God's faith."*

This may not seem significant, and doesn't change Christ's emphasis on the need for faith, but it does serve to remind us as to where such mountain-moving faith comes from. And it's also possible, He may have been describing a special spiritual gifting of faith, that He grants for particular situations or moments *(1 Corinthians 12:9)*. Nonetheless, Jesus was telling his disciples to look to God as their all-sufficient source of faith, reassuring them of His unlimited power to rearrange things, regardless of whatever need or mountainous challenge they might face.

Were Jesus' remarks meant to be taken literally or figuratively? I believe they were both. He certainly wanted to widen the eyes of His disciples, by providing an extreme example of what God-given faith could be capable of. Obviously, such faith could "potentially" move actual mountains if warranted by the Lord for some reason, but Jesus was primarily referring to mountains in a figurative sense. He was illustrating that no mountain or "problem" is too extreme for God and us to remove, if we can believe Him and not doubt.

Jesus is the source, the author and finisher of our faith, and when our prayers and faith is based upon Him and what He has promised, we can be confident and assured that He will be faithful to bring such things to pass. *"Therefore I say to you, whatever things you ask when you pray, believe that you receive them, and you will have them" (Mark 11:22-24).*

So did Jesus literally mean for us to speak to things? Apparently so, since that's what He did himself on many occasions. Such as the time he and the disciples were sailing across the Sea of Galilee, and a sudden storm nearly sank their boat. To their shock, He rebuked the wind and waves, and spoke to the sea to become still (*Mark 4:39-41*).

Over and over again, throughout His ministry, Jesus spoke to things, to spirits and illnesses with authority. He laid hands on and declared healing to the sick, commanded demons to depart, and even told dead persons to come back to life.

For example, for a deaf and mute child who was afflicted by a demon, He said, *"Deaf and dumb spirit, I command you, come out of him and enter him no more!"* and the spirit departed (*Mark 9:25*). When a leper who came to Him, asking whether it was His will to make him clean, Jesus put out His hand and touched him, saying, *"I am willing; be cleansed"* and he was immediately healed (*Matthew 8:3*). To a shouting man who had a demon, Jesus said *"Be quiet, and come out of him!" (Luke 4:35).*

In other examples, such as a widow, whose son had just died, Jesus touched the coffin, and said, *"Young man, I say to you, arise."* And he rose up alive and began to speak (*Luke 7:15*). For a woman who had been crippled and bent over for 18 years, He said to her, *"Woman, you are loosed from your infirmity,"* and when He laid His hands on her, she was made straight (*Luke 13:13*). For a man who had been disabled for 38 years, Jesus said to him, *"Rise, take up your bed and walk" (John 5:8),* and he did so and was healed. For two blind men, who cried out to Him for mercy, the Bible says *"Jesus had compassion on them and touched their eyes. Immediately they received their sight and followed him" (Matthew 20:34).*

Jesus, however, is not the only one who ministered this way, but also his disciples. When Peter saw a crippled man begging by the beautiful gate, He made the famous declaration, *"Silver or gold I do not have, but what I have I give you. In the name of Jesus Christ of Nazareth, walk"* *(Acts 3:6)*. Then taking him by the right hand, he helped him up, and the man's feet and ankles became strong and healed. In another instance, he was asked to come pray for a Christian woman who had died. He asked them all to leave the room; then he knelt and prayed. *"Turning to the body he said, Get up, Tabitha. And she opened her eyes! When she saw Peter, she sat up! He gave her his hand and helped her up. Then he called in the widows and all the believers, and he presented her to them alive"* *(Acts 9:40-41)*.

And of course, the miracles that followed Paul were numerous, such as the girl with a spirit of divination who followed and annoyed his ministry. He eventually turned to her, and said *"I command you in the name of Jesus Christ to come out of her. And he came out that very hour"* *(Acts 16:16-18)*. And there was a lame man in Lystra, who had never walked. As he heard Paul's preaching, Paul discerned he had faith to be healed, and declared, *"Stand up straight on your feet! And he leaped and walked"* *(Acts 14:8-10)*. And God did many other unusual miracles through Paul's ministry, *"so that even handkerchiefs or aprons were brought from his body to the sick, and the diseases left them and the evil spirits went out of them"* *(Acts 19:11-12)*.

Faith and Authority During an Emergency

One of my earliest encounters with this kind of prayer, occurred one day when I was suddenly faced with an emergency. My mom had been struggling with illness for quite some time, but suddenly collapsed and started to bleed profusely. We immediately prayed for her until the bleeding subsided, but we knew we needed to get her to the hospital quickly from our rural home.

I ran out to the car to bring it to our front porch, but to my shock it wouldn't start! I had no idea if the battery was dead or what, but repeated attempts got no results. I calmed down briefly and remembered what I had been learning about spiritual authority and our warfare against Satan in Ephesians 6:12. It occurred to me that the Devil was behind this, and was trying to destroy my mom's life.

So, as I called upon Jesus, and prayed fervently for a few moments, a strong feeling of faith, along with anger at the Devil suddenly rose up in me. With all the authority I could muster, I rebuked Satan and commanded the car to start "in the name of JESUS!" Then I turned the key again, and it started right up! We quickly loaded mom into the car and got her to the hospital, and she lived several more years before Lord finally took her home.

Ministering with Faith and Authority

Years later, as my wife I answered God's calling to serve in Gospel ministry, we found ourselves in many other situations to pray with similar faith and authority. We discovered that under the anointing and direction of the Holy Spirit, the Lord would often use us this way to pray for the sick, and sometimes even to bring deliverance to persons troubled by demonic spirits.

One especially notable instance of healing, occurred as we were conducting special meetings for a small church in the Midwest. During the second night of services, I felt inclined to ask persons forward who would like prayer for healing, but no one responded except for one young mother and her little boy, about 8 or 9 years old.

I had never met them, nor did I know anything about their need, but learned that the child had been deaf since he was a baby. I could also tell something about the mom and her faith without being told. Her tear-filled eyes seemed to sparkle with optimism, and I could sense that she had been praying and believing God for a miracle for a long time. As I laid my hands on the child's ears, I asked the congregation to agree with us in prayer... then I lifted my voice and said to the boy, *"In the name of Jesus Christ, I command these ears to open!"*

The moment I said this, a surprised look came across the little boy's face. I clapped my hands, and he appeared even more shocked. He looked at his mother, nodded his head up and down and began to cry. She began weeping too, and said, *"He can hear!"* To be sure, I walked behind him, clapped my hands and spoke words, and he continued nodding, and his mother confirmed that he could hear for the first time!

It was a remarkable miracle that we could never forget. And over the years, we've witnessed this type of miraculous response to prayer on many occasions, although not always. There's a lot of factors involved with praying for others, since God is dealing with each person in a special and individual way.

Among other things, while the faith of the persons praying is important, so is the faith of the person being prayed for. We're reminded that even Jesus, when He returned to minister in his hometown, Nazareth, He was unable to many great things, because of their unbelief *(Matthew 13:58)*.

Also, though God may use the prayer or spoken words of preachers or ministers, they are not the healer, God is, and all the glory and credit goes to Him *(Revelation 4:11)*. While a minister may be used by Gifts of the Holy Spirit to be a part of such astonishing things, they merely give voice to the Lord's Will and Words, lending their hands to serve as His for a time.

And finally, we should also remember that whomever God chooses to preach His Word or bring His healing or deliverance's, they still are only human beings, not perfect in any way. This means they can still make mistakes, commit sin or even backslide. So don't put your eyes on them. Keep your eyes on Jesus *(Hebrews 12:2)*.

And He said to them, "Go into all the world and preach the gospel to every creature. He who believes and is baptized will be saved; but he who does not believe will be condemned. And these signs will follow those who believe: In My name they will cast out demons; they will speak with new tongues; they will take up serpents; and if they drink anything deadly, it will by no means hurt them; they will lay hands on the sick, and they will recover. So then, after the Lord had spoken to them, He was received up into heaven, and sat down at the right hand of God. And they went out and preached everywhere, the Lord working with them and confirming the word through the accompanying signs" (Mark 16:15-20).

37. What Does It Mean to Pray in the Spirit?

Praying in the Spirit essentially means to pray according to the will of God by the leading, assistance or the power of the Holy Spirit. There are moments that we especially need the Holy Spirit's help in our prayers, and the Apostle Paul says that He can make intercession for us when we don't know how to pray.

"Likewise the Spirit also helps in our weaknesses. For we do not know what we should pray for as we ought, but the Spirit Himself makes intercession for us with groanings which cannot be uttered. Now He who searches the hearts knows what the mind of the Spirit is, because He makes intercession for the saints according to the will of God" *(Romans 8:26-27).*

Such prayer comes from the depths of our soul, with passion and fervency, often accompanied with expressions of worship, weeping or by praying in tongues, which Paul specifically associated with praying in the spirit. He said, *"For if I pray in tongues, my spirit is praying"* ... *(1 Corinthians 14:14 NLT).*

Paul was a strong advocate for believers to be filled with the Spirit *(Ephesians 5:18)*, as well as to speak/pray in tongues *(1 Corinthians 14:5)*, which he claimed to exercise more than anyone else *(1 Corinthians 14:18)*. But he also seemed to suggest that prayer in the Spirit could occur without utterances... or even with groanings, which some have described as travailings. Perhaps this explains the groaning of Jesus in John 11:33, as a travail of His spirit for Lazarus, who had died before Jesus could return to the home she shared with his sisters, Mary and Martha.

The purpose of praying in the Spirit is for the Holy Spirit to assist us in moments of need, that our prayers might be more effectual by praying in accordance to God's will. The objective is not necessarily to exhibit exuberant or strange behavior. However, this is something that can occur whenever persons become deeply immersed in the presence of the Holy Spirit. Just as early believers spoke in other tongues and appeared intoxicated when the Holy Spirit descended in the upper room *(Acts 2:4-15)*, similar patterns may occur whenever human frailty is overwhelmed by the Spirit's presence.

Such was the pattern of two ministers named Daniel Nash and Abel Clary, intercessors who accompanied the famed evangelist, Charles Finney.[1] Finney was one of the most powerful and effective evangelists in America's 19th century (and eventual president of Oberlin College). He believed that before revival could come to any community, it first needed prepared and saturated with prayer... and he knew of none as powerful and effective in prayer than these two men of God.

Nash and Clary were sent ahead of Finney by several days, to gather a few others to pray with them until the revival meetings would begin. And later, during the meetings, they continued their prayers in a separate place, continually interceding for Finney and the outpouring of God's Spirit upon him. The results of their prayers speak for themselves, as thousands came to the meetings and were converted to Christ.

Nash was a former pastor who, for some time, had given himself to almost continual prayer... rising often before dawn to pray in the woods or nearby church. As the Holy Spirit came upon him in prayer, his groanings and travail often became so intense, that nearby families had sometimes reported hearing what they thought was an escaped lunatic roaming the countryside.

Clary was also a preacher, but would become so overwhelmed with a burden for prayer, that he could rarely complete a sermon. While in the pulpit, he would often begin moaning in his spirit and be unable to stand under the fervor and passion that came upon him. As they came together with Finney's ministry, Nash and Clary spent most of their time fasting and praying... often weeping, groaning and crying out to God, sometimes lying prostrate without strength to stand up.

Later, as Finney reflected on the way his intercessors would pray by the unction of the Spirit, he recounted, *"On one occasion when I got to the town to start a revival a lady contacted me who ran a boarding house. She said, 'Brother Finney, do you know a Father Nash? He and two other men have been at my boarding house for the last three days, but they haven't eaten a bite of food. I opened the door and peeped in on them because I could hear them groaning and I saw them down on their faces. They have been this way for three days, lying prostrate on the floor and groaning. I thought something awful must have happened to them. I was afraid to go in and I did not know what to do. Would you please come see about them? No it is not necessary, I replied. They just have the Spirit of Travail in prayer,"* (an obvious reference to Romans 8:26) *"the Spirit making intercession for us with groanings which cannot be uttered."*[2]

Prayer in the Spirit is important for many reasons, beginning with His assistance to coordinate our prayers with the will of God *(Romans 8:26-27)*. However, Paul also taught that praying in the Spirit has an edifying effect on a believer's faith *(Jude 1:20)*, and is significant to our warfare with the Devil. And he encouraged believers to "always" incorporate this practice in their prayer lives. *"Pray in the Spirit at all times and on every occasion. Stay alert and be persistent in your prayers for all believers everywhere" (Ephesians 6:18 NLT).*

[1] *Daniel Nash 1775-1831 – Prayer Warrior for Charles Finney, by J Paul Reno, 2013*
[2] *Fresh Wind, Fresh Fire, By Jim Cymbala*

38. What is the Prayer of Jabez?

This refers to the simple, yet inspiring prayer of a Bible character named Jabez, which has often been the subject of sermons, as a model of humility and reliance on God. *"There was a man named Jabez who was more honorable than any of his brothers. His mother named him Jabez because his birth had been so painful. He was the one who prayed to the God of Israel, Oh, that you would bless me and expand my territory! Please be with me in all that I do, and keep me from all trouble and pain! And God granted him his request" (1 Chronicles 4:9-10 NLT).*

Since the Bible doesn't mention Jabez elsewhere, we really don't know much about him, except that he was from the tribe of Judah, probably a son of Koz, and for some unstated reason was considered more honorable than his siblings. He also apparently caused his mother great distress during childbirth, since she named him Jabez, which literally means "pain and sorrow" in the Hebrew.

Obviously, people had different ideas about naming children back then, as I can't imagine anyone naming their child "a pain." However, it appears his name may have played a part in his prayers, in that among other requests, he also asked the Lord to keep him from pain, or as some translations say, "from causing pain."

As I've pondered Jabez and his prayer, I suspect he must have grown up with a sense of humiliation and suffering each time he heard his name called, a continual reminder that his entry into the world had brought pain to his mother. And I think that this may have contributed to the humility and simple motives seen in his prayer, that while he asked the Lord to bless him with expanded territory and divine favor, he did not want this at the expense of causing pain or sorrow to anyone, nor to himself.

We certainly can sympathize with Jabez, as it would seem an injustice for any child to grow up with such an embarrassing derogatory name. But in his case, it doesn't seem to have made him bitter, but may have actually helped shape his character toward a more humble and submissive soul. Jabez not only had a solid faith in the God of Israel, but also trusted the Lord to be with him in all areas of his life.

This reminds us that when believers face ordeals, trials and injustices in life, they always have a choice to make with how they respond *(James 1:2-4)*. They can either grow resentful toward unfairness, and distance themselves from the God who allowed it... or else fall at His feet in worship and submission, trusting in His will and fate for their lives, as Job said, *"Though He slay me, yet will I trust Him..." (Job 13:15)*.

God apparently found pleasure with Jabez' faith *(Hebrews 11:6)*, as well as his character, motives and attitude, inasmuch that he granted his request, to bless him and enlarge his boundaries. Thus, the prayer of Jabez serves as a model to all believers, to humble ourselves before God and trust Him no matter what.

"Therefore humble yourselves under the mighty hand of God, that He may exalt you in due time, casting all your care upon Him, for He cares for you" (1 Peter 5:6-7).

39. What does it mean to "Pray-Through?"

This is an old term, rarely mentioned or heard of in churches anymore... but is something that definitely needs to be rekindled by contemporary believers. While the term doesn't originate from scripture, it emerged as a description of "persevering" prayer, such as when Jacob wrestled all night in prayer, until he received blessing from God *(Genesis 32:26)*.

To "pray-through" means to pray until a "breakthrough" comes... either the answer itself, or perhaps until you experience a peace or assurance that God has undertaken in your behalf. There is no set time involved with "praying-through," but it generally implies that schedules or other routines are set aside temporarily... that the only thing of immediate importance is the burden to keep praying, often accompanied with fasting, to press through until obtaining the desired result.

In today's short-attention, drive-through type of thinking, the idea of intense prolonged prayer, may seem bizarre or foreign, but I believe this a major reason why many believers have failed to get answers to prayers... or have fallen short of transformative spiritual experiences. I have often heard people say, since God didn't answer their prayer, it must not have been His will... and have just accepted that as their result. Unfortunately, this lack of spiritual determination by the church has left it impaired and deficient from the ideals that God has for it.

However, if the Bible promises something that we have failed to receive or experience, we shouldn't give up praying, believing or pursuing that goal, but should rather press in with greater determination, faith and persistence. As much as possible, we should set aside special moments to do nothing more than pray and fast, to seek God's help and intervention... as He promised to those *"who diligently seek Him"* in faith *(Hebrews 11:6)*.

To illustrate this point, let me use an example of something that often needs this kind of prayer by many in the church. Though secular society calls alcoholism a disease, the Bible refers to it as a work of the flesh called "drunkenness." Drunkenness is listed together with other sins like murder and adultery, practiced by those whom the scriptures say will not inherit the kingdom of God *(Galatians 5:19-21)*.

The Apostle Paul considered drunkenness among professing Christians to be so serious, that he warned us not to keep company, nor even eat a meal with drunkards who profess to be believers. *"When I wrote to you before, I told you not to associate with people who indulge in sexual sin. But I wasn't talking about unbelievers who indulge in sexual sin, or are greedy, or cheat people, or worship idols. You would have to leave this world to avoid people like that. I meant that you are not to associate with anyone who claims to be a believer yet indulges in sexual sin, or is greedy, or worships idols, or is abusive, or is a drunkard,*

*or cheats people. Don't even eat with such people" (1
Corinthians 5:9-11 NLT).*

Consequently, if drunkenness is considered so critical to
one's Christian walk, the believer should see it as
something that needs repented of and forsaken from their
lifestyle at all costs. And while this might not be difficult
for some, it may be more challenging to others who are
literally addicted to alcohol. But God's Word tells us that
Christ provides us the power to overcome this or any sin
or addiction *(John 1:12)*. We just have to stand our ground
in faith and determination to procure it through prayer!

This is precisely the kind of situation where a believer
needs to pray-through. Of course, we applaud self-
determination, programs or medical methods of
withdrawal. But over the centuries, thousands have come
to Christ, relying only on God's strength in prayer to turn
away from sin and such bondages. Over the years as a
pastor, I've known many who have prayed-through until
receiving their deliverance... and I have prayed with many
new converts at the altar, interceding for them until they
achieved victory over this or other addictions.

Praying-through applies to any issue that needs persistent
faith and determination. Set aside a day or more to do
nothing else but fast and pray. Repeat these vigils as
necessary, and keep praying in faith daily, "all the way
through," until you receive the assurance of your answer
or breakthrough from God. *"...do not become sluggish, but
imitate those who through faith and patience inherit the
promises" (Hebrews 6:12).*

This is where church prayer meetings are especially
important and powerful, as others pray with you,

interceding and "persevering" until an answer comes. *"...if two of you agree on earth concerning anything that they ask, it will be done for them by My Father in heaven" (Matthew 18:19).*

40. Is Intercession the Same Thing as Prayer?

Intercession means to "plead in behalf of another." Therefore, when the object of prayer is an appeal for God to help other people, this falls into the category of intercession. All believers are called to intercede for one another, such as the Apostle Paul told Timothy, *"I urge you, first of all, to pray for all people. Ask God to help them; intercede on their behalf, and give thanks for them" (1 Timothy 2:1 NLT).* Also, to the church at Ephesus, Paul wrote, *"Pray in the Spirit at all times and on every occasion. Stay alert and be persistent in your prayers for all believers everywhere" (Ephesians 6:18 NLT).*

In another instance, Paul wrote of his intercession for the believers at Colossae, *"For this reason we also, since the day we heard it, do not cease to pray for you, and to ask that you may be filled with the knowledge of His will in all wisdom and spiritual understanding" (Colossians 1:9).* He also requested their intercession for him, *"that God would open to us a door for the word, to speak the mystery of Christ" (Colossians 4:3).* And apparently, Epaphras, a colleague of Paul's in Rome, was also quite an intercessor, of whom Paul wrote, *"He is always wrestling in prayer for you, that you may stand firm in all the will of God, mature and fully assured" (Colossians 4:12 NIV).*

Another great example of intercessory prayer is seen when the Jerusalem church interceded for Peter after he was arrested and jailed for preaching the Gospel. *"Peter was therefore kept in prison, but constant prayer was offered to God for him by the church" (Acts 12:5)*. Herod had already put James to death, and wanted to try and execute Peter as well, but decided to wait a few days since this was during the time of the Jew's Passover feast. Meanwhile, as the church prayed desperately for Peter around-the-clock, an astonishing miracle occurred in Peter's prison cell. An Angel appeared to him, causing the chains to fall off his hands, and the iron city gate opened by itself as the Angel led him from the prison *(Acts 12:1-11)*. This is the kind of power that God can still release today, if the body of Christ will only pray and seek God.

Intercessors are important because prayer is the means God uses to work in the behalf of others. While Jesus is the only mediator between God and man, standing at God's right hand interceding for us *(1 Timothy 2:5, Romans 8:34)*, believers also serve as intermediaries to intercede and help reconcile souls to the life-changing truths of Jesus *(2 Corinthians 5:18)*. In other words, the prayers of an intercessor helps "bridge the gap" in behalf of others... taking up the slack, adding strength to theirs, helping them make a connection. *"I sought for a man among them who would make a wall, and stand in the gap before Me on behalf of the land, that I should not destroy it; but I found no one" (Ezekiel 22:30)*.

Intercession is something that all Christians are called to participate with... however some believers feel a special calling, passion or anointing toward intercessory prayer and consider that their primary ministry. While prayer isn't specifically mentioned as a gift in scripture, "faith" certainly is *(1 Corinthians 12:9)*, as well as other motivational-type gifts such as such as service, mercy or helps *(Romans 12:3-7)* ... any of which may involve this kind of intercessory prayer.

Most everyone has heard of Dr. Billy Graham, the famed Gospel Evangelist of the 20th century. But while he was known around the world, and preached to millions through crusades and television... far fewer ever heard of Pearl Goode. She was a 65-year-old widowed grandmother from Pasadena, California, whose ministry of prayer and intercession under-girded Graham's successful ministry for decades.

Goode, along with fellow believers, started interceding privately for Billy Graham during his first Los Angeles crusade in 1949, something that wasn't new to her. Pearl had developed a passion for prayer and intercession from the age of seventeen, shortly after her conversion to Christ in the Methodist Church. She would often spend days and nights fasting and praying for a variety of needs. *"The old Methodists taught that, and I was trained that way and I saw it in the Bible,"* she said.[1]

According to Graham's longtime associate, Cliff Barrows, Goode was an unusually devoted intercessor, who felt called, not only to pray, but to teach and to train others how to pray and intercede.[1] Before her intercession for Graham's crusades, she often hosted informal prayer seminars in her home for ministerial students from nearby Fuller Seminary, teaching them about the ministry of prayer.

Initially, Graham and his team were unaware of Goode's intercessions during the Los Angeles crusade. They only knew God was blessing in an extraordinary way, insomuch that the nightly meetings extended from three weeks to eight. The crowds even swelled into the many thousands. However, behind the scenes Goode, along with scores of other believers, had privately organized informal groups who were praying and fasting around the clock for the success of the crusade.

Then as all this was going on, something else unexpected occurred that changed everything for Graham's ministry. For unknown reasons, newspaper magnate, William Randolph Hearst, decided to promote the story of Graham's crusade across his chain of twenty-eight major newspapers. Virtually overnight, the relatively unknown Billy Graham became a national sensation.

"Puff Graham," was the message Hearst dispatched to his editors, who readily understood that Graham was to receive top publicity. Their reports were then picked up by the Associated Press, and forwarded as lead stories to hundreds of other cities. Time, Life, Newsweek, and other national magazines gave as much as four pages to it. Even Shanghai's Communist-censored English newspaper carried it on page one.

Neither Goode, nor any of her intercessors, ever sought credit for their part in the marvelous things God did in Los Angeles, but all those involved, especially Graham, eventually came to realize the significance of her ministry. But before they did, she had already been interceding for Graham for years, following the crusades to most of their scheduled U.S. cities.

Goode didn't actually attend the crusade services themselves, but made arrangements to stay in an area home or in a room by herself, where she would spend days praying and fasting for the city, for Graham's team, and for the receptiveness to the Gospel message. During the crusades she prayed fervently for Graham as he preached. She would cry out to the Lord, asking Him to pour out His Spirit on Graham as he preached the cross, and for souls to respond and get saved.

Until she began traveling by airplane in later years, Pearl Goode rode buses to the crusades at her own expense, logging more than 48,000 miles on Greyhound. While she remained unknown for most of her years of intercession, Graham's team finally discovered what she was doing, and began providing her travel and accommodations to the various cities. They realized her prayers, along with those she organized, were playing an important role in the success of the crusades. She continued her prayer ministry until her death in 1972.

Without a doubt, Pearl Goode's intercessory prayers, along with the prayers of many others, were a vital part of what God used to help Billy Graham succeed in leading throngs of souls into the kingdom of God. Graham never met William Randolph Hearst, nor ever learned why he received such favor, but only knew that the blessing came from God in response to the many prayers of intercessors such as Pearl Goode.

Graham was a praying man and always valued the importance of such intercession, but after learning about the amazing role that Goode and her prayer warriors played in his success, he made sure such intercession was given greater priority. For the remainder of his crusade years, each of his meetings were bathed in advance by organized round-the-clock prayer gatherings, with thousands of intercessors asking God to anoint the crusades and to open the hearts of lost souls.

But long before Billy Graham, there were other especially anointed Gospel preachers who also knew the value of intercessory prayer. One of these was a converted lawyer named Charles Finney, who became the most prominent evangelist of the nineteenth century... as well as one of the most important figures of his era. During an age without sound systems, radio or television, Finney preached to some of the largest crowds ever gathered up to that time.

While Finney was quite well-known, Daniel Nash and Abel Clary, were relatively unknown ministers of prayer who accompanied the evangelist as his intercessors.[2] Finney believed that a community first needed cultivated with prayer before his ministry could be effective, so he dispatched Nash and Clary in advance, who would seek a few others to intercede with them until revival meetings began. And even during the meetings as Finney preached, they continued praying in a separate place, calling on the Lord to pour out His Holy Spirit. As a result, more than a half-million souls came to Jesus Christ though Finney's meetings.

What we know for sure is that the prayers of intercessors are vital to the work of God and the success of the Gospel. As important as preaching is to the ministry, it cannot produce results without the power and anointing of the Holy Spirit... which requires the foundation of fervent prayer and intercession.

While their labors have often gone unseen in the background, intercessors have literally laid the foundation for the success of their church or pastor, working hand-in-hand with the invisible agents of God's forces, while wrestling with evil unseen principalities and powers. For this reason, intercessors are sometimes also referred to as "spiritual warriors," as God gives them a faith willing to engage spiritual battles... praying persistently for victory, despite the challenges of spiritual conflict, doubt, persecution, that Satan inspires or exploits to oppose Christians from receiving God's help *(Ephesians 6:12, 2 Corinthians 10:4-5)*.

[1] *Transcript of Pearl Goode interview, Billy Graham Center Wheaton College, 1970*
[2] *Passion for Souls, Passion for Prayer, Cliff Barrows, Billy Graham Evangelistic Association, 2005*
[3] *Daniel Nash 1775-1831 – Prayer Warrior for Charles Finney, by J Paul Reno, 2013*

41. What is Spiritual Warfare?

Spiritual warfare is essentially a believer's fight of faith against the spiritual forces of our adversary, Satan. The Devil is always attempting to hinder, distract, or instigate temptations or trials, hoping to exploit possible spiritual weaknesses to undermine our faith. And the believer prepares and responds to such assaults with spiritual weaponry... the exercise of prayer, faith, spiritual authority, and such things that strengthen our faith and relationship to God.

Although much of Satan's mischief is easily recognized, most of his activity is clandestine, hidden in the shadows, as he uses subtlety, deceit and manipulation behind the scenes. He attempts to disguise his sabotage with subtle whispers into our thoughts, or by seductive temptations to entice our flesh, or through the actions of other people.

For example, we may remember the incident when Peter challenged Christ's prediction of His approaching sufferings and death, and Jesus rebuked him, saying *"Get behind Me, Satan!" (Matthew 16:23).* Peter was not possessed by the Devil, but Satan definitely inspired his thoughts and words, bringing a sharp rebuff from the Lord.

Because the Devil often seeks to exploit the careless words or behavior of people around us, even those of fellow Christians or members of our family, Paul warns us to be especially on guard against such ploys, and to remember who our real enemy is. *"For we do not wrestle against flesh and blood, but against principalities, against powers, against the rulers of the darkness of this age, against spiritual hosts of wickedness in the heavenly places" (Ephesians 6:12).*

And since such struggles come from spiritual sources, they must also be fought by spiritual means. The devil's mischief cannot be overcome with conventional weapons, nor can we end his resistance by sparring with the people or vessels that he exploits. Satan can only be defeated by the spiritual arsenal that God makes available to believers. *"For the weapons of our warfare are not carnal but mighty in God for pulling down strongholds, casting down arguments and every high thing that exalts itself against the knowledge of God, bringing every thought into captivity to the obedience of Christ" (2 Corinthians 10:4-5).*

The Apostle Paul explained that our greatest defense against Satan, is to *"be strong in the Lord and in the power of His might" (Ephesians 6:10).* And he used the description of a soldier's battle gear, as a metaphor of God's armor that believers should put on and wear.

He said, *"...put on every piece of God's armor so you will be able to resist the enemy in the time of evil. Then after the battle you will still be standing firm. Stand your ground, putting on the belt of truth and the body armor of God's righteousness. For shoes, put on the peace that comes from the Good News so that you will be fully prepared. In addition to all of these, hold up the shield of faith to stop the fiery arrows of the devil. Put on salvation as your helmet, and take the sword of the Spirit, which is the word of God. Pray in the Spirit at all times and on every occasion. Stay alert and be persistent in your prayers for all believers everywhere"* (Ephesians 6:13-18 NLT).

These items, along with all resources that strengthen our faith and spiritual life, are essential to our arsenal, and can be summarized into three essential phases of spiritual warfare:

(1) Submission to the Lord – The necessity of our submission to God is obvious, as His Holy Spirit is the source from which we draw our strength, as Jesus said, *"...without Me you can do nothing"* (John 15:5). Such submission, however, also involves surrendering "self" to Him... that is our "fleshly nature," that tends to struggle against God's desires, and which Satan targets with his temptations and manipulations. *"So humble yourselves before God. Resist the devil, and he will flee from you. Come close to God, and God will come close to you. Wash your hands, you sinners; purify your hearts..."* (James 4:7-9 NLT).

Humbling ourselves before the Lord, confessing and forsaking sin *(1 John 1:9)*, and maintaining a repentant heart of obedience toward righteousness, is the way to resist the Devil. When Satan can find nothing in us that will pay attention or cooperate with him, he'll withdraw at least for a temporary season. *(See also 2 Timothy 2:3-4, and 1 John 2:15-16).*

(2) Faith in God's Word – Equally indispensable to our warfare, is the application of faith in God's Word, as Paul said to *"Fight the good fight of faith..." (1 Timothy 6:12 NKJV).* You may recall how Jesus used the written Word of God in His defense against the Devil's temptations in the wilderness *(Matthew 4:1-11).* In each instance, Jesus squashed the assault by quoting scripture. For instance, when tempted to turn stones to bread at the conclusion of His 40-day fast, he responded by quoting from Deuteronomy 8:3, *"It is written, Man shall not live by bread alone, but by every word that proceeds from the mouth of God" (Matthew 4:4).*

God's Word, the sword of the Spirit, is both a defensive and offensive weapon against Satan, that proclaims our authority and victory over the Devil. Among other assurances, Jesus explained that God's indwelling Spirit in His followers, made them greater than the influence of Satan in the world. *"...He who is in you is greater than he who is in the world" (1 John 4:4).* Jesus also made a declaration of the believer's authority over the Devil... not only to serve as a defense, but to enable His followers to take the offensive... to remove and expel his evil works through faith in His name. *"Behold, I give you the authority to trample on serpents and scorpions, and over all the power of the enemy, and nothing shall by any means hurt you" (Luke 10:19).*

(3) Prayer and Intercession – When we speak of spiritual warfare, it's with the understanding that there are many important spiritual aspects involved, but nothing any more essential than prayer.... praying not only for our own lives, but also interceding for other believers. Prayer and faith are the primary means by which believers wage war against the Devil. Prayer is the application of faith that leads the way... the component that God needs in order to intervene and act on our behalf. And while we engage the spiritual battle on our knees in prayer, God is able to dispatch His angels to confront and push back the forces of darkness in our behalf.

(4) Spiritual Authority – When Jesus was confronted by Satan's ploys and temptations, He countered with stern rebukes and the Word of God. *"Jesus answered and said to him, Get behind Me, Satan! For it is written, You shall worship the Lord your God, and Him only you shall serve" (Luke 4:8).* This same authority over the Devil, has been given to all followers of Christ, to repel and rebuff his evil influence from our lives and ministry. *"Behold, I give you the authority to trample on serpents and scorpions, and over all the power of the enemy, and nothing shall by any means hurt you" (Luke 10:19).*

When you perceive Satan's involvement in such assaults or persistent problems, by faith exercise your authority over him and his wicked forces. Stand your ground, declare the authority of God's Word, and demand him to depart... and he will ultimately yield to your persistence and faith. But don't make the mistake of focusing on the Devil's distractions. Command him and his demons to leave, but rely on the Lord's unseen angelic army to enforce the authority of your faith, and wage victory over the enemy's conflicts. In the meantime, keep praying and maintain your attention on the Lord, from whom comes your faith and spiritual strength, and whose very presence repels the forces of darkness.

Combat in the Spiritual Realm

While we are unable to see such things with our natural eye, scripture indicates that when we pray, the forces of God actually wage war in our behalf against the forces of Satan in the unseen spiritual realm. An example of this is revealed from the story of Daniel's prophetic visions and his prolonged prayers for their meaning. After praying for twenty-one days, an angelic visitor made a surprise visit to Daniel.

The angel not only brought the interpretation that Daniel had been praying for... but also explained that he had been delayed due to resistance from the spirit prince of the kingdom of Persia. And in order to prevail in this conflict, he had to call for the help of the mighty archangel, Michael. *"Since the first day you began to pray for understanding and to humble yourself before your God, your request has been heard in heaven. I have come in answer to your prayer. But for twenty-one days the spirit prince of the kingdom of Persia blocked my way. Then Michael, one of the archangels, came to help me..." (Daniel 10:12-13 NLT).*

Another example is shown during the time that the king of Syria was at war with Israel and plotted to capture of Elisha. His servant rose one morning and panicked when he saw the shocking scene of enemy troops, horses, and chariots gathered around them. But Elisha reassured him that God's unseen forces with them, outnumbered those against them. *"Don't be afraid!' Elisha told him. 'For there are more on our side than on theirs!' Then Elisha*

151

prayed, 'O Lord, open his eyes and let him see!' The Lord opened the young man's eyes, and when he looked up, he saw that the hillside around Elisha was filled with horses and chariots of fire" (2 Kings 6:16-17 NLT).

Even though we may not see anything when we pray, understand that God responds to our faith and engages the powers of darkness in our behalf. And our continued prayers of faith are vital for His angelic forces to continue waging their battle against our enemy. Don't give up, don't quit praying or believing... but continue with confidence that the answer is on its way!

42. Can Prayer Make the Devil Leave Me Alone?

Combined with other spiritual components, such as submission to God, and the application of faith and spiritual authority, **prayer can enable the believer to rise in victory against the various assaults, temptations or harassments of the Devil.** Jesus demonstrated His power over Satan during His earthly ministry. And through the triumph of His death and resurrection, He extended His authority over the Devil to all believers who have His Indwelling Spirit.

However, even though the Lord intends for you to be victorious over Satan, this doesn't necessarily mean that he will ever completely "leave you alone." Even though Jesus always walked in victory over the devil and his temptations, Satan continued to pose many trials, hindrances and challenges... and left Jesus alone only for temporary "seasons," returning to pester Him frequently. *"Now when the devil had ended every temptation, he departed from Him until an opportune time" (Luke 4:13).*

What Jesus experienced will not be unlike the scenario that you and I will face. Though every believer can remain strong and overcome whatever mischief Satan may bring, we must be prepared to contend with him daily, and never let our guard down... as he never withdraws his influence permanently. Satan will always be nearby, looking for any opportunity, foothold, or even the slightest prospect of weakness, that he can use to tempt or exploit against you. One of his favorite tactics, in fact, is to pull back a while to give believers the "illusion" that they have no need to pray... so to lull them into apathy, or to occupy them with careless living or the pleasures of this world. Don't be fooled!

When you find yourself harassed by the devil, the first thing you should do is to seek the Lord and His strength to rise against the enemy's challenge *(James 4:7-8)*, and utilize the spiritual weapons and authority He provides to use against the enemy *(Ephesians 6:10-18)*. Regardless of the circumstances, or people that might be involved, always be aware that your conflict is not with "human beings" *(Ephesians 6:12)*, but with wicked spiritual entities which must be resisted and overcome by spiritual means. *"For the weapons of our warfare are not carnal but mighty in God for pulling down strongholds" (2 Corinthians 10:3-4).*

Resisting the devil always involves drawing closer to God, and by submitting yourself to Him. As scripture says, *"Submit yourself to God. Resist the devil and he will flee from you. Draw near to God and He will draw near to you" (James 4:7-8).* Please note that James describes this as something a believer must take the initiative to do. Obviously, the Holy Spirit is always at work, drawing you toward the Lord *(John 6:44)*, but no one can submit

153

yourself to God, except you. And when you reach out to pull yourself toward Him, He will draw near to you.

How to Resist the Devil

(1) If you are aware of unconfessed sin in your life, it needs to be submitted to God through repentance. The devil will always make a claim against anyone who walks in sin, immorality or disobedience to God *(James 4:4, 1 John 2:15)*. Confessing and forsaking sin withdraws such vulnerabilities that Satan can use against you. When you receive God's forgiveness by faith, and turn away from sin, Satan is disabled from using that as a means to pull you down. This applies what Paul described as the *"breastplate of righteousness" (Ephesians 6:14)*, which protects your vital resources from the Devil's assaults.

(2) Submit yourself to God though prayer, worship, feeding on His Word, and fellowshiping with believers. If you neglect these spiritual resources, you will grow weak spiritually... something that Satan keeps a close eye on, hoping he can trip you up during such times. This submission is a part of taking on the "armor of God," to strengthen yourself against your enemy. Paul wrote, *"Finally, my brethren, be strong in the Lord and in the power of His might. Put on the whole armor of God, that you may be able to stand against the wiles of the devil. For we do not wrestle against flesh and blood, but against principalities, against powers, against the rulers of the darkness of this age, against spiritual hosts of wickedness in the heavenly places. Therefore take up the whole armor of God, that you may be able to withstand in the evil day, and having done all, to stand" (Ephesians 6:10-13)*.

154

(3) Finally, by faith, exercise your right as a follower of Christ to use the authority of Jesus' name, to repel or rebuff the assaults of the Devil. This means that if or when you experience Satan's oppressions, pray and verbally "rebuke" or command the devil to depart from you, by using the name and authority of your Lord Jesus *(Mark 16:17, Luke 10:17).* If you recall, this push-back, along with quoting from the written Word of God, is how Jesus responded when He was tempted by the devil in the wilderness *(Matthew 4:1-11).* Jesus wielded the authority of God's Word against the Devil, by proclaiming scripture. Each time that He countered Satan's temptations, He quoted from the Torah, saying *"It is written."* Notice the references from Deuteronomy in brackets, that indicate what Jesus was quoting from below.

"Then Jesus was led up by the Spirit into the wilderness to be tempted by the devil. And when He had fasted forty days and forty nights, afterward He was hungry. Now when the tempter came to Him, he said, If You are the Son of God, command that these stones become bread. But He answered and said, <u>It is written,</u> Man shall not live by bread alone, but by every word that proceeds from the mouth of God" *[Deuteronomy 8:3].*

"Then the devil took Him up into the holy city, set Him on the pinnacle of the temple, and said to Him, If You are the Son of God, throw Yourself down. For it is written: He shall give His angels charge over you, and, In their hands they shall bear you up, Lest you dash your foot against a stone. Jesus said to him, <u>It is written again,</u> You shall not tempt the Lord your God" *[Deuteronomy 6:16].*

"Again, the devil took Him up on an exceedingly high mountain, and showed Him all the kingdoms of the world and their glory. And he said to Him, All these things I will give You if You will fall down and worship me. Then Jesus said to him, Away with you, Satan! <u>For it is written</u>, You shall worship the Lord your God, and Him only you shall serve" [Deuteronomy 6:13].

"Then the devil left Him, and behold, angels came and ministered to Him." (Matthew 4:1-11).

One other thing. As I've shared elsewhere in this writing, the focus of your attention must never become centered on the Devil or his activities. Believers engaged in spiritual conflict sometimes mistakenly give too much attention to Satan, which only feeds a trap of diverting your attention away from power and presence of Christ. Order the devil to skedaddle, but redirect your focus back toward the Lord and keep it there. Satan hates the presence of Christ-centered worship, spirit-filled prayer and the reading or proclaiming of God's word.

43. Can Bad Things Happen to People Who Pray?

Believers who live for the Lord and pray in faith, can expect God to answer their prayers and bring His intervention, provision and blessings. But this doesn't mean that they'll ever be exempt from problems or the possibility of calamity or tragedy. Scripture says that the *"rain falls upon the just and unjust" (Matthew 5:45),* and those who follow Christ will also experience many temptations and trials... some so severe that their faith may be tested to its limit.

Something believers can be sure of, is if we have trusted Christ with our life, He is in charge of everything that happens to us... and even though there may be moments of great difficulty, He promises at least three things:

(1) That He will not allow anything to come upon us that is more than we can bear. *"No temptation has overtaken you except such as is common to man; but God is faithful, who will not allow you to be tempted beyond what you are able, but with the temptation will also make the way of escape, that you may be able to bear it" (1 Corinthians 10:13).*

(2) That "all things," whether good or bad, will work together for a good result in our life. *"And we know that all things work together for good to those who love God, to those who are the called according to His purpose" (Romans 8:28).*

(3) That He will eventually answer our cry to deliver us from our afflictions, either by removing them, and/or by giving us the peace and strength to endure. *"The righteous cry out, and the Lord hears, And delivers them out of all their troubles. The Lord is near to those who have a broken heart, And saves such as have a contrite spirit. Many are the afflictions of the righteous, But the Lord delivers him out of them all" (Psalms 34:17-19).*

As we have said, temptations and trials are common to all believers, because they are necessary components to our faith in God. Faith that is untested, is not really worth anything... any more than raw gold ore that has not yet been purged and refined in the smelting furnace. Thus, trials serve that purpose, of testing and refining our faith, as the Apostle Peter wrote, *"greatly rejoice, though now for a little while, if need be, you have been grieved by various trials, that the genuineness of your faith, being much more precious than gold that perishes, though it is tested by fire, may be found to praise, honor, and glory at the revelation of Jesus Christ" (1 Peter 1:6-7).*

Many of those to whom Peter wrote, seemed surprised by the persecution and trials they experienced, as though they didn't expect their faith to be contested or challenged. However, this must be anticipated. *"Beloved, do not think it strange concerning the fiery trial which is to try you, as though some strange thing happened to you; but rejoice to the extent that you partake of Christ's sufferings, that when His glory is revealed, you may also be glad with exceeding joy" (1 Peter 4:12-13).*

Whenever you pray and apply faith in God for any reason, you must expect your faith to be contested by doubt, unbelief, or by Satan causing delays or complications. In his devotional, *My Utmost for His Highest*, Oswald Chambers wrote, *"Faith must be tested, because it can only become your intimate possession through conflict... Believe steadfastly on Him and everything that challenges you will strengthen your faith."*[1]

One of the most extreme examples of faith tested, can be seen in the life of Job, described the biblical book bearing his name. While the kind of ordeals that befell Job may not be typical of the daily problems most believers face, all of God's children will experience temptations and trials, some so severe that their faith will be pushed to the edge.

According to scripture, Job was the wealthiest man of his region and had a remarkably blessed life. He was also an outstanding follower of the Lord, *"blameless and upright, and one who feared God and shunned evil" (Job 1:1).* And ironically, it's for that reason, he was singled out and allowed to be tried by the devil.

Once God gave Satan permission to try him, Job essentially began experiencing the loss of everything he had, including his health, the support of his friends and even his wife. We don't how long the ordeal lasted, but scripture only refers to months *(Job 7:3)*, while Jewish tradition suggests a year or longer.

First, Job's 1000 oxen and donkeys were stolen and his servants were killed *(Job 1:14-15)*. Fire then fell from the sky and consumed his 7000 sheep, killing more of his servants *(Job 1:16)*. Then his 3000 camels were stolen, and even more of his servants were killed *(Job 1:17)*. Following this, a great wind destroyed a house, killing Job's 7 sons and 3 daughters *(Job 1:18-19)*. (Whew! It exhausts me just to recount all this calamity!)

And what was Job's response? He grieved deeply over the awful things that were happening, but he refused to blame God in the least. *"Job stood up and tore his robe in grief. Then he shaved his head and fell to the ground to worship. He said, I came naked from my mother's womb, and I will be naked when I leave. The Lord gave me what I had, and the Lord has taken it away. Praise the name of the Lord!" In all of this, Job did not sin by blaming God" (Job 1:20-22 NLT).*

But the ordeal was not yet over. Job was then smitten from head to toe with painful boils *(Job 2:7)* which caused fever and blackened his skin *(Job 30:30)*. And although he was incapacitated, rather than encouraging him his wife then traumatized him further with criticism. She even told him to give up... to curse God and die (incidentally, she is never mentioned again).

And finally, Job is visited by three so-called "friends" who add to his distress by piling on with false accusations and judgmentalism. Eliphaz accused Job of harboring secret sin as the reason for his calamities *(Job 4:7)*, Bildad similarly accused Job, even suggesting that his children had also been to blame *(Job 8:4)*. And Zophar was even more condemning, calling Job a liar for defending himself *(Job 11:3-4)*, and referring to him as "wicked" and a "hypocrite." They obviously hurt Job deeply, who called then "miserable comforters," and replied, *"How long will you torment my soul, And break me in pieces with words?" (Job 19:2)*.

Job lost everything... the lives of his 10 children, all his livestock, all but 4 of his servants, his health, the respect and support of his wife and friends. And if it ended this way, this would be a dismal story, but thank God, it didn't.

Despite everything, Job never lost his integrity (Job 2:3), never cursed or spoke improperly against the Lord *(Job 2:10, Job 42:8)* and held steadfast to his faith and trust in God *(Job 13:15)*. **And because of his faithfulness, God not only restored, but multiplied everything he had lost *(Job 42:12-13)*.**

Interestingly, God finally *"turned the captivity of Job"* and brought the ordeal to an end, when Job "prayed for his friends" who had been so brutal and condemning *(Job*

42:10). I've always suspected that the emotional toll from these false comforters, may have been the most difficult thing he endured. And by choosing to pray for them, and not allowing himself to become bitter, put himself over the top in God's eyes. *"And the Lord restored Job's losses when he prayed for his friends. Indeed the Lord gave Job twice as much as he had before" (Job 42:10).*

This is the amazing part of this... and the lesson we learn about trials. Not only did God restore Job, but He doubled what he had before... even his years of life upon the earth. It's believed that Job was around 70 when his testing began, and lived 140 more years. *"Then all his brothers, sisters, and former friends came and feasted with him in his home. And they consoled him and comforted him because of all the trials the Lord had brought against him. And each of them brought him a gift of money and a gold ring. So the Lord blessed Job in the second half of his life even more than in the beginning. For now he had 14,000 sheep, 6,000 camels, 1,000 teams of oxen, and 1,000 female donkeys. He also gave Job seven more sons and three more daughters" (Job 42:11-13 NLT).*

The history of Job's life shows us that even the most devoted followers of the Lord are not exempt from the possibility of horrendous trials or difficulty. However, we also know that God will not allow us to suffer anything without purpose, and will use whatever challenges to help make us stronger and to bring about promotion in the end. *"And we know that God causes everything to work together for the good of those who love God and are called according to his purpose for them" (Romans 8:28 NLT).*

"Though the mills of God grind slowly, yet they grind exceeding small; Though with patience He stands waiting,

with exactness grinds He all." -- Henry Wadsworth Longfellow

[1] *The Unsurpassed Intimacy of Tested Faith, My Utmost for His Highest, Oswald Chambers, 1935*

44. Will God Give Me a Thorn in the Flesh Like Paul?
(Trials, Tribulations and Persecutions)

While it is true that God permitted a *"Thorn in the Flesh"* to afflict the Apostle Paul, one should first understand that the Lord dealt with him as one of His most anointed and privileged apostles, unlike most of us. Among other things, God blessed Paul with astonishing revelations, even translating him to Paradise where he heard things not allowed to be repeated on the earth *(2 Corinthians 12:1-4)*. The signs and wonders that followed his ministry were so remarkable, that many would lay their sick loved-ones along his path, so that if only touched by his shadow, they might receive a miracle *(Acts 5:15)*. Even mere handkerchiefs or cloths passed from his body, would bring healing or deliverance *(Acts 19:11-12)*.

Thus, to help keep him humble, the Lord allowed the Devil to bring a (limited) measure of resistance against him. Paul said, *"...So to keep me from becoming proud, I was given a thorn in my flesh, a messenger from Satan to torment me and keep me from becoming proud"* (2 Corinthians 12:7 NLT).

This probably came as quite a shock to Paul at first. He had become accustomed to seeing remarkable results from his prayers... healings, miracles, casting out evil spirits, exercising authority over the Devil. But now, he was likely confounded as to why the Lord was allowing these torments in his life. This was especially disturbing, since many of these afflictions (his thorns in the flesh) were severe. Persecutions, stonings, beatings, scourgings, shipwrecks and other assorted troubles *(2 Corinthians 11:22-33, Acts 14:19)*.

When the Lord responded to Paul, explaining that the "thorn in his flesh" was allowed to keep him from becoming proud, it probably helped ease his concerns. But the Lord also added something else that seemed to strike a special chord. Paul said, *"Three different times I begged the Lord to take it away. Each time he said, 'My grace is all you need. My power works best in weakness...'" (2 Corinthians 12:8-9 NLT)*.

When Paul heard this, he caught sight of the greater purpose behind this. He was aware of his need for continual humility... and realized that the Lord was allowing such assaults and afflictions to keep him on his knees, so he would keep increasing in God's power and strength. This reminds me so much of what Smith Wigglesworth once said, *"A man is in a great place when he has no one to turn to but God,"[1]*

When a believer has nowhere else to turn, nor can do anything to save himself from crisis, that's when his faith and trust in God can reach its greatest potential. Paul replied, *"...So now I am glad to boast about my weaknesses, so that the power of Christ can work through me. That's why I take pleasure in my weaknesses, and in the insults, hardships, persecutions, and troubles that I suffer for Christ. For when I am weak, then I am strong" (2 Corinthians 12:9-10 NLT)*.

Few of us may ever suffer the extremes that Paul did, however these same basic principles apply to all of us. Crisis or affliction tends to draw people of faith closer to the Lord. None of us want troubles to come our way, but desperate situations generally motivate us to pray and reach out to God with greater intensity, devotion and fervor. Like Oswald Chambers wrote, *"We do not pray at all until we are at our wits' end."*[2] This kind of intensity can be seen in the prayer of David as he cried out for God's help. *"Listen to my cry, for I am in desperate need; rescue me from those who pursue me, for they are too strong for me" (Psalms 142:6 NIV).*

Thus, we can see the benefit of tribulations, trials and persecution. These kinds of conflicts will be frequent in a believer's life. But if we can embrace the value of their resistance, and respond in prayer and faith like Paul did, they can help bring us closer to the Lord. His power and strength in us can become amplified to greater levels during our vulnerable moments of need and affliction. Such as it did for Abraham Lincoln, during the horrible conflict of the Civil War. He said, *"I have been driven many times upon my knees by the overwhelming conviction that I had nowhere else to go."*[3]

Paul's Thorn in the Flesh reveals an important truth, that God will not allow such troubles to come our way, except for our benefit. And like Paul, we should gladly embrace the "opportunities" that such trials give us... so to "fight the fight of faith," to wage war against spiritual conflict. Because we know when we resist and pray in faith, we will eventually rise above the challenges and grow stronger in God's power! As James wrote, *"Dear brothers and sisters, when troubles come your way, consider it an opportunity for great joy. For you know that when your faith is tested, your endurance has a chance to grow. So let it grow, for when your endurance is fully developed, you will be perfect and complete, needing nothing" (James 1:2-4 NLT).*

So did Paul resist the "thorn in the flesh" that God allowed to afflict him? Absolutely, otherwise it would have served no benefit. The Messenger of Satan was not sent to destroy him, but to oppose and "buffet" him... giving him opportunity to resist and overcome. Paul had to fight tooth and nail to maintain his steadfastness through prayer and faith, which is what made him stronger in the Lord. It kept him on his knees as a yielded and humble servant, increasing his dependence on the sustaining power of his Lord and Savior.

Although it appears that these "thorns in the flesh" never left Paul entirely, he held fast to his victory by faith, and never allowed it to diminish his confidence. He wrote, *"We are hard pressed on every side, yet not crushed; we are perplexed, but not in despair; persecuted, but not forsaken; struck down, but not destroyed-- always carrying about in the body the dying of the Lord Jesus, that the life of Jesus also may be manifested in our body" (2 Corinthians 4:8-10).*

So, will God allow you to be afflicted with this same "thorn in the flesh?" It's not likely. This thorn was something extreme, assigned specifically for the Apostle Paul. It was to suppress his pride in light of such extraordinary revelations and anointing. However, trials, tribulations and persecutions WILL come your way, which will be allowed to test your faith and provide opportunities for you to resist, and fight the *"fight of faith" (1 Timothy 6:12).*

165

Don't make the mistake that some have made, to let troubles and difficulties to diminish your faith, or to make you bitter or resentful. Trials don't come to destroy you... but only to make you better, to draw you closer, to make you stronger in Christ our Lord. Like Paul, be glad and "embrace" the opportunity for your faith to be tested... so your prayers can grow in the strength and power of God.

"So be truly glad. There is wonderful joy ahead, even though you have to endure many trials for a little while. These trials will show that your faith is genuine. It is being tested as fire tests and purifies gold—though your faith is far more precious than mere gold. So when your faith remains strong through many trials, it will bring you much praise and glory and honor on the day when Jesus Christ is revealed to the whole world" (1 Peter 1:6-7 NLT).

[1] *Wigglesworth on the Anointing, by Smith Wigglesworth, 1947*
[2]*The Purpose of Prayer, My Utmost for His Highest, Oswald Chambers, 1935*
[3]*Lincoln Observed: The Civil War Dispatches of Noah Brooks edited by Michael Burlingame*

45. How Can I Have a More Passionate Prayer Life?

One of my most life-changing experiences with prayer, occurred one Sunday night when I was just twelve years old. While our family watched television together, we were unaware that our rural Indiana farmhouse was in the direct path of a rapidly approaching twister that had already killed thirteen local residents.

As soon as my parents saw the TV tornado alert, they directed us to take shelter in the basement... and only minutes later, the tornado's thundering winds collided

with our home. The structure shook violently with the
noise of breakage and groans of twisted timbers. And yet
in the background, I remember also hearing my mother's
pleas, praying and calling out to the Lord for His help.
"Dear Jesus, please help us! Dear Jesus, please help us!"
she kept repeating.

My mom's prayer was the first I can ever recall of
someone praying so intently as though their life depended
on it... which God apparently heard and answered, saving
our lives. And while there was destruction all around our
house, we were unharmed and our home was left largely
intact. I was stunned later when a neighbor told me how
he watched the twister rise over our house and come back
down on the other side, which coincided with the exact
moment of my mom's passionate prayers!

There may be things that none of us may fully understand
about prayer, but I can definitely attest to the fact that
God pays close attention to the desperate, faith-filled
prayer of a godly person. As James wrote, *"...The effective,
fervent prayer of a righteous man avails much" (James
5:16).* Such prayers often emerge from urgencies that
cause believers to drop everything else, to pray
passionately and unashamedly... as though their life, or
the life of a loved one, depends upon it.

This kind of passion was likely what the late Leonard
Ravenhill meant, when he said, *"God doesn't answer
prayer. He answers desperate prayer!"*[1] And in the words
of pastor/author, Jim Cymbala, *"When God is sought in
desperation, he responds. Even in hopeless situations."*[2]

Author E.M. Bounds, also offered what might be one of
the most eloquent descriptions of passionate prayer,

undoubtedly shaped by his prior perspective as a chaplain in the Confederate army. Among his many heart-wrenching experiences, he comforted scores of wounded and dying soldiers who prayed and called out to God in the trenches during the horrific Battle of Franklin, one of the bloodiest battles of the Civil War. He wrote, *"Prayer must be aflame. Its ardor must consume. Prayer without fervor is as a sun without light or heat, or as a flower without beauty or fragrance. A soul devoted to God is a fervent soul, and prayer is the creature of that flame."*[4]

The question is, however, how can we pray with this same desperation, even if a tornado isn't barreling down on us... or if our life doesn't depend on it? There are legitimate matters that are deserving of our ardent prayers, even though they may not always rise to the level of life and death.

I can remember many of my past attempts to arouse the need for prayer in church members, who were unable to see the urgency of lost souls, or the crisis of spiritual opposition that we faced as a church. I've also personally struggled at times to pray passionately for things that I knew needed the fervent attention of my prayers, but I could not bring myself to that level of urgency.

Unfortunately, as long as things are going well, without any urgent crises or problems, many Christians can easily fall into a slumbering state of passivity or apathy... unable to perceive or realize the need for urgency.

While preaching about this matter years ago, I made the facetious remark, *"We need to do something to wake ourselves up, to see the need, to realize how urgent our prayers are needed. Maybe like taking a 16-ounce hammer and slamming it down hard on our big toe!"*

Folks laughed, but it brought home an important point. We all must find a way to stay stirred up with a need to pray, and we can't wait for anyone else to do it for us. That is, we must all take responsibility for stirring ourselves up, instead of passing the buck on to the pastor or somebody else to stir us. As Paul said, *"I remind you to stir up the gift of God which is in you..." (2 Timothy 1:6).*

Steps to Renew Your Prayer Passion

(1) Dwell and Meditate on God's Word – People often lack a burden for souls or other spiritual priorities, because they've become distant from the Gospel and the purpose for why Jesus willingly suffered and died on the Cross. Keeping your thought-life focused on God and His Word, instead of the cares and distractions of this world, will help feed your faith and stir your spiritual man with the kind of inspiration and passion you need to pray effectively. *"Let the words of my mouth and the meditation of my heart Be acceptable in Your sight, O Lord, my strength and my Redeemer" (Psalms 19:14).*

(2) Maintain a Regular Regimen of Prayer – Spiritual passion can be interpreted as something fiery or excited, but can also be understood as persistence and determination. Remember, it's easier to build a bonfire on top of smoldering embers than on cold wet wood.... and if you get a fire going, just keep pouring on fuel and don't let it go out. Your persistence to pray faithfully is the framework on which passion can grow to support an even more powerful and vibrant prayer life. *"Evening and* *morning and at noon I will pray, and cry aloud, And He shall hear my voice" (Psalms 55:17).*

(3) Fast and Pray – Combining the Biblical discipline of "fasting" together with our prayers, is an important and valuable spiritual practice. Among other things, fasting is a voluntary form of self-denial and humility before God. It helps to arouse a sense of urgency or need... that helps stir the sincerity and intensity of our prayer life. *"Now, therefore, says the Lord, Turn to Me with all your heart, With fasting, with weeping, and with mourning" (Joel 2:12).*

(4) Pray in the Spirit – This is one of great reasons that believers need to be filled with the Holy Spirit, so that His indwelling presence may help pray in our moments of need or distress. The Holy Spirit is our comforter and helper, who enables and equips us with the power to serve God and live the Christian life. *"...the Spirit also helps in our weaknesses. For we do not know what we should pray for as we ought, but the Spirit Himself makes intercession for us with groanings which cannot be uttered" (Romans 8:26).*

(5) Exploit your Trials – Many believers have a faulty understanding of the purpose of trials, viewing them only as annoyances and distractions. However, troubles and difficulties are "opportunities" for our faith and spiritual passions to grow. The problems that burden us and drive us to our knees, help us to pray and appeal to God with depth and sincerity. Such persistence against opposition, discouragement or doubt, can help build our faith and spiritual strength. *"My brethren, count it all joy when you fall into various trials, knowing that the testing of your faith produces patience. But let patience have its perfect*

*work, that you may be perfect and complete, lacking
nothing" (James 1:2-4).*

(6) Pray Together with Other Believers – There is no
substitute for a personal private prayer life with the Lord,
but having frequent opportunities to pray with other
believers is also absolutely essential. Such prayer adds to
our faith and spiritual encouragement, provides examples
for how to model our own prayers, and acts upon the
promise of God's Word... that Jesus will manifest His
presence, and honor their prayers of agreement between
each other.

My view is that all Bible-believing churches should have
prayer meetings. And all believers should attend, both to
encourage, and be encouraged. *"Again I say to you that if
two of you agree on earth concerning anything that they
ask, it will be done for them by My Father in heaven. For
where two or three are gathered together in My name, I am
there in the midst of them" (Matthew 18:19-20).*

[1] *Prayer, Leonard Ravenhill, 1995*
[2] *Storm: Hearing Jesus for the Times We Live In, Jim Cymbala, 2014*
[3] *Our Ultimate Refuge: Job and the Problem of Suffering, Oswald
Chambers, 1935*
[4]*The Essentials of Prayer, E.M. Bounds, 1922*

46. Can We Pray for the Devil to Go to Hell?

I wish we could simply send the Devil to the pit and be
done with him, but unfortunately, that's not possible in
this present time. Satan is already condemned and will
eventually be cast into Hell, but such prayers will not
expedite his arrival. At the very end of this age, after the
millennial reign of Christ during which Satan is bound,

the Devil will be loosed again for a brief season. But then he will "finally" be thrown into the lake of fire, from which he will never again emerge. *"The devil, who deceived them, was cast into the lake of fire and brimstone where the beast and the false prophet are. And they will be tormented day and night forever and ever" (Revelation 20:10).*

Many wonder why Satan still roams the earth causing havoc, or why God allows him to exist. These are challenging questions, but I can at least offer a few explanations that should help one's understanding.

The Bible tells us that the Devil, or Satan, originated as Lucifer, one of the three archangels of heaven. But because of his wicked attempt to rebel and overthrow the Lord, he along with his other fallen angels (what we now refer to as demons) were expelled from Heaven, and cast down to the earth *(Isaiah 14:12-15, Revelation 12:7-9).* While the destination of the Devil and will "eventually" be the lake of fire *(Matthew 25:41),* he is not there yet. The Bible explains that Satan presently roams the earth, as an unseen spirit personality, seeking to tempt, hinder or destroy the lives of those who put their faith in God.

Jesus described the Devil as a "thief," whose only goal is to "steal, and to kill, and to destroy..." *(John 10:10),* however scripture also refers to Satan by a variety of other titles... such as a Liar and Murderer *(John 8:44),* the Evil One *(John 17:15),* the Ruler of Darkness (Ephesians 6:12), the Ruler of this world *(John 12:31),* the Ruler of demons *(Luke 11:15),* the Wicked One *(Ephesians 6:16),* the Deceiver (Revelation 12:9), the Enemy *(Matthew 13:39),* the Tempter *(Matthew 4:3)* and the Adversary of believers.

Peter even describes the Devil like a "Roaring Lion," reminding us that we live where Satan prowls about, and must always be alert and prepared for his continual efforts to destroy us. *"Be sober, be vigilant; because your adversary the devil walks about like a roaring lion, seeking whom he may devour" (1 Peter 5:8)*. But notice, Peter isn't saying he really is such a lion, but only that he "roars" and "imitates" one... as an attempt to intimidate us and make us fearful.

This of course is just another of the Devil's lies, as with Christ in our heart, we are far more powerful than Satan. Jesus overcame the Devil, and when His Spirit comes into the heart of a believer, He also brings His same authority and power over Satan. As Jesus said, *"He who is in you is greater than he who is in the world" (1 John 4:4)*.

So, if the presence of Christ in the believer, is greater than the power of the Devil, why should we have any concern with him at all? Simply for this reason... the Devil is very sly and cunning, and uses lies, deception and manipulation of the carnal/sensual nature, as a strategy to outwit Christians. Yes, as astonishing as this sounds... Satan's primary weapon against believers is "deception!" He attempts to disguise his activities behind other people or things *(Ephesians 6:12)*, sometimes masquerading as a false minister, or even an "angel of light" *(2 Corinthians 11:13-14)*. The Devil is the ultimate con-man, who bluffs, lies, and deceives Christians into fear and intimidation.

Without a doubt, pulling ourselves closer to God through prayer is a vital part of the believer's defensive arsenal, that allows the Lord to strengthen our resistance against Satan's ploys and assaults. However, prayer alone is not enough to overcome all the enemy's tactics. James said that to resist the devil, we must also submit our "self" nature to God... because our "flesh" is the primary target of Satan's temptations and manipulations. *"Therefore submit to God. Resist the devil and he will flee from you. Draw near to God and He will draw near to you" (James 4:7).*

Submitting our "self" to the Lord, involves the idea of surrendering our life to the Lordship of Jesus... while also "crucifying" or "dying" to the old sinful desires of the flesh. *".... those who are Christ's have crucified the flesh with its passions and desires" (Galatians 5:24).* "Crucifying the flesh" is a metaphor to describe the idea of smothering the flesh's influence, so that it's lusts and passions no longer rule over us.

When we become a believer, Christ's Holy Spirit comes into our heart, and we begin a new life of yielding ourselves "daily" to the leadership of His Spirit... who also gives us the strength to deny the influence of the sinful flesh that formerly ruled our thinking and the way we lived. *"Therefore, dear brothers and sisters, you have no obligation to do what your sinful nature urges you to do. For if you live by its dictates, you will die. But if through the power of the Spirit you put to death the deeds of your sinful nature, you will live. For all who are led by the Spirit of God are children of God" (Romans 8:12-14 NLT).*

Ever since he Garden of Eden, the Devil has found his way of influence into man's life through his weaker flesh nature. Thus, to remain strong against the ploys of the enemy, we must feed on those things of Christ that nourish our spiritual nature, while starving or "putting to death" those things that feed the lusts and passions of the flesh nature. *"If then you were raised with Christ, seek those things which are above... therefore put to death your members which are on the earth: fornication, uncleanness, passion, evil desire, and covetousness, which is idolatry" (Colossians 3:1,5).*

The Apostle Paul also describes an array of spiritual "armor" that Christians must wear and use, to assure victory over Satan's evil assaults *(Ephesians 6:10-18).* Paul's point was to emphasize the reality that all believers are in a battle with the Devil, and that it will take everything at our disposal, to overcome. *"Therefore take up the whole armor of God, that you may be able to withstand in the evil day, and having done all, to stand" (Ephesians 6:13).*

In Ephesians 6:14-18, Paul used the metaphor of a soldier's armor (probably a Roman soldier), to illustrate these spiritual virtues and weaponry that every believer should be equipped with: The Belt of Truth (verse 14), The Breastplate of Righteousness (verse 14), Gospel Footwear (verse 15), The Shield of Faith (verse 16), The Helmet of Salvation (verse 17), The Sword of the Spirit (verse 17) along with the persistent prayers for our fellow believers in the body of Christ (verse 18).

But despite the fact that we can "overcome" the devil, doesn't mean that he vanishes and no longer bothers us. When Jesus went to the wilderness to fast and pray for forty days, as described in Matthew chapter 4, the Devil showed up to tempt and annoy Him. The first time I read this as a new believer, I was shocked to see Satan's person-to-person visitation and conversation with Jesus, whom the Devil tempted three times. And how did Jesus respond? By using the sword of the Word of God, just like we must do when attacked or tempted by the Devil.

The Devil first tempted Jesus, (1) to satisfy his earthly appetites by turning stones to bread, but Jesus responded, *"It is written, Man shall not live by bread alone, but by every word that proceeds from the mouth of God" (Matthew 4:4)*.

Then the Devil tempted Him again, (2) to throw himself down from a high place, as a prideful display of His power and prominence when upheld by the Angels. Jesus replied, *"It is written again, You shall not tempt the Lord your God" (Matthew 4:7)*.

Lastly, the Devil tempted Him a third time, (3) by offering him vast power and rulership over the earth... if only He would simply bow down and worship Satan. *"Then Jesus said to him, Away with you, Satan! For it is written, You shall worship the Lord your God, and Him only you shall serve" (Matthew 4:10)*.

Finally, after this, the devil left Him (for a season) and the angels came and ministered to Him *(Matthew 4:11)*.

Unfortunately, during this lifetime, we will never be able to eradicate the Devil completely. He will always be nearby, lurking, watching for opportunities, seeking weakness to exploit... but we do not have to fall as prey to His devices, nor be overcome by his temptations or deceptions.

So be filled with the Holy Spirit *(Ephesians 5:8)*, put on the Christian's armor that the Lord has provided *(Ephesians 6:10-18)*, and be quick to do as Jesus did when assaulted and tempted by Satan... to declare and exercise the powerful sword of God's Word, that will thwart the Devil's plans, and bring refreshing strength and encouragement from God's presence.

"For the word of God is living and powerful, and sharper than any two-edged sword, piercing even to the division of soul and spirit, and of joints and marrow, and is a discerner of the thoughts and intents of the heart" (Hebrews 4:12).

47. Can Prayer Cast Out Demons?

Yes, the prayer of a believer or believers, combined with faith and the authoritative use of the name of Jesus, can expel demons. Jesus said this is one of the supernatural signs that would accompany His followers. *"And these signs will follow those who believe: In My name they will cast out demons..." Mark 16:17).*

People often assume that expelling demons should be left up to ministers or those who specialize in such "deliverance" ministries. However, just imagine the strategic advantage this can provide to demons, if they know that they'll not be displaced until someone else is found to come deal with them. That would be like a burglar who knows he'll not be confronted by a homeowner, so he breaks in with little concern that he'll be apprehended later by the police.

Obviously, there are ministers especially experienced or gifted with bringing deliverance... and if you're faced with such issues, it would be wise to seek their assistance, or learn from their experience. But all truly born-again believers have the right to assert the authority of the name of Jesus, to repel, remove and extract the powers of darkness... and may eventually find themselves in a predicament where they must do so.

In fact, in one of the Gospel's most remarkable passages, Jesus explained to a group of his disciples, that the most marvelous thing about their authority over demon spirits, was the fact that it bore evidence that their names were written in heaven! *"Then the seventy returned with joy, saying, 'Lord, even the demons are subject to us in Your name.' And He said to them, 'I saw Satan fall like lightning from heaven. Behold, I give you the authority to trample on serpents and scorpions, and over all the power of the enemy, and nothing shall by any means hurt you. Nevertheless do not rejoice in this, that the spirits are subject to you, but rather rejoice because your names are written in heaven'" (Luke 10:17-20).*

What Jesus was saying, is that because the names of His followers are written in the Lamb's book of life *(Revelation 21:27)*, they, including YOU, have power over the Devil and his forces in Jesus' name! This is an awesome revelation to understand!

However, don't take anything for granted when dealing with Satan, as He is a formidable adversary who will look for any loophole, weakness or advantage to exploit you. In other words, when dealing with this enemy, a believer must draw close to Christ in prayer, faith, repentance, and be filled with His Spirit... and take on God's full array of weaponry, to be effective. *"Finally, my brethren, be strong in the Lord and in the power of His might. Put on the whole armor of God, that you may be able to stand against the wiles of the devil" (Ephesians 6:10-11).*

Needless to say, dealing with the devil or casting out demons is not something for non-believers... nor for "nominal" Christians, who ascribe to Christianity, but without the experience of the new birth. In this modern

era in which fewer people seem to understand authentic
Christianity, there are many who "allege" to be Christ's
followers, yet without the indwelling of His Spirit. If
these, or any other so-called religious persons attempt to
confront genuine demonic forces, they will be putting
themselves at great risk of possible harm... or at the least,
will be ineffectual in bringing any helpful results.

As an illustration of this, the book of Acts describes the
attempt of Jewish leaders, including seven sons of a chief
priest named Sceva, who attempted to expel a demon by
using the name of Jesus "whom Paul preaches," but with
disastrous results.

*"Then some of the itinerant Jewish exorcists took it upon
themselves to call the name of the Lord Jesus over those
who had evil spirits, saying, 'We exorcise you by the Jesus
whom Paul preaches.' Also there were seven sons of Sceva,
a Jewish chief priest, who did so. And the evil spirit
answered and said, 'Jesus I know, and Paul I know; but
who are you?' Then the man in whom the evil spirit was
leaped on them, overpowered them, and prevailed against
them, so that they fled out of that house naked and
wounded"* (Acts 19:13-16).

As we have said, only if a person's name is recorded in
Heaven, will such persons have the right to exercise the
authority of Jesus' name. And to be sure, Satan and his
demons "know" those in whom Christ dwells, and tremble
at the power at their disposal.

My advice for believers who may face such things, is to
draw close to the Lord Jesus through repentance,
humility, prayer and fasting. Be full of the Holy Spirit,
and equip yourself with the armor of faith in God's Word,

and you'll be prepared should you be confronted with demons or the power of darkness.

Use caution, however, from presuming that every problem or issue is a demon. Some people get carried away and start seeking demons everywhere. Obviously, Satan and his forces have an indirect influence on a great many things, but not everything. Demons often attempt to hide themselves, such as submerged in a person's personality... but when confronted with spirit-filled believers, or an anointed atmosphere of worship, prayer, preaching... they'll often manifest or expose themselves, which is usually the moment of opportunity to cast them out in the name of Jesus.

In my experience, I've never felt the need to go hunting after demons. But whenever anyone pursues a spirit-filled ministry of the Gospel, sooner or later they'll generally be confronted with instances where they'll need to expel demonic forces, as I describe from this incident some years ago.

My wife and I were just concluding the final service of a week of revival meetings in a central-Illinois church, when men unknown to us appeared at the rear of the sanctuary, asking to speak with the pastor. After talking a few moments with the gentlemen who appeared distressed, the pastor urgently motioned for me to come join him, and we followed the men out the door and down the street toward another church about a block away.

Along the way, the men explained that they were elders of their church, currently without a pastor, and a stranger had come into their service moments earlier, displaying all sorts of bizarre behavior which they believed to be demonic. They and the people of their congregation were alarmed, but rather than call the police, they came next door to see if we could help offer a spiritual solution.

As the pastor and I walked into their church, we soon discovered that the elders were right to be concerned. There standing at the altar, surrounded by perhaps fifteen or twenty frightened church members, was a wild-looking young man in disheveled clothing, flailing his arms about, while growling, barking and cursing. As we approached the group, this man whom we had never met, stopped his antics for a moment and angrily asked, "why have these men of God come?" (This is a good sign whenever demons recognize who you are, and acknowledge that God is inside you.)

A look of shock came on the pastor's face. *"I've heard about such things, but have never seen anything like this before,"* he said. Looking at me, he asked *"Do you know what to do?"* *"Yep, I've dealt with this before... it appears to be a demon or demons, and we're going to need to cast them out,"* I said.

So for the next hour or so, the pastor and I, along with the elders and others in their congregation gathered around the man, praying for his deliverance. I directed the group to join hands and pray, and to sing songs like *"Oh the Blood of Jesus,"* as I laid hands on the man, commanding the demons to come out "in the name of Jesus." I asked the others to simply pray, not to scream or yell, nor direct their comments to the man or demons... but to let just one leader, myself in this case, do the talking.

Each time I would command the demons to come out, the man's eyes would roll, his tongue would protrude, and he would writhe, flail and curse as though he were suffering a seizure. Frequently the demons would scream or speak out with different voices, cursing and threatening us, or pleading with us to stop... but we didn't cease until the man was finally set free and resumed a normal personality. Once we felt confident that he was free from demons, we then led the man into a prayer of repentance, to receive Jesus as his savior and to fill his heart with Christ's presence. Satan or his demons cannot rule where Jesus is Lord!

Please note, you may sometimes hear reports from secular news media about bizarre exorcism attempts. I've sometimes heard of goofy people who try to "beat" the devil out of persons, or perhaps restrain them in an attempt to force their cooperation. Such tactics are illegal, unscriptural, and are unproductive. Jesus never had to beat up or handcuff anyone to deal with demons. If a believer truly has the indwelling of the Holy Spirit, demons will recognize their authority, and will respond (although reluctantly) to persistent commands in the name of Jesus.

In this confrontation, it was helpful to have the combined faith and spiritual support of this pastor, as well as several other strong believers. My preference has always been to keep a deliverance of this kind in a private setting, but it doesn't always work out that way. Jesus frequently cast out devils in plain sight during his public ministry. It might seem shocking for those who have never witnessed such a thing, but it usually promotes a sobering awareness of Satan's reality, as well as God's power and authority over the Devil.

As we have often said, believers need always to be "prayed

up," walking in close fellowship with the Lord Jesus, so that when faced with evil forces at a moment's notice, we can be confident of our authority and power in Christ. Never forget, *"...He who is in you is greater than he who is in the world" (1 John 4:4).*

48. Can Prayer Break a Spell or Curse on Me?

Yes, prayer, combined with a strong relationship with Jesus and the application of other spiritual regimen such as fasting, can be effective in breaking evil associations of this nature. Although such concerns are often over-exaggerated by superstitions or unwarranted fears, there really are legitimate curses. Many of these actually originate in the bible, but many others come from sorcery, such as incantations, spells, hexes, instigated by persons who participate with the occult or witchcraft.

The Bible explains that sorcery is an evil practice that originates with Satan, and those who perform such things are an abomination to the Lord. *"And do not let your people practice fortune-telling, or use sorcery, or interpret omens, or engage in witchcraft, or cast spells, or function as mediums or psychics, or call forth the spirits of the dead. Anyone who does these things is detestable to the Lord..." (Deuteronomy 18:10-12 NLT).*

I'll address more about this sort of thing later, but for now, the kind of curses to be most concerned about, are those that the Bible refers to, beginning with the curse of sin and death that all mankind contends with. Understanding this curse, and how it's power has been broken over the believer through Christ, will help you to overcome all other curses.

This curse exists because of the sin and disobedience by our first parents, Adam and Eve. As a result, sin and death became the nature passed on to all their descendants *(Genesis 3:1-24, Romans 5:12)*. Therefore, regardless whether anyone realizes it or not, people are already cursed as soon as they enter the world because of their inherited sinful nature. Sin not only brings the curse of physical death, but also eternal spiritual death, which is a never-ending existence of darkness and torment. This horrible fate will to be shared with Satan in a place of punishment that was created for him and his demons.

However, the great news of the Gospel, is that Jesus willingly gave His own life on the cross as your substitute, taking the curse of sin and death upon Himself. So, by believing upon Him and His atoning sacrifice, you are set free from the horrible consequences of this curse. *"But Christ has rescued us from the curse pronounced by the law. When he was hung on the cross, he took upon himself the curse for our wrongdoing. For it is written in the Scriptures, Cursed is everyone who is hung on a tree"* *(Galatians 3:13 NLT)*.

In other words, when you receive Christ as your Lord and Savior, He brings forgiveness of your sins and the promise of salvation, which sets you free from the curse of sin and death. And very importantly, this also severs the effects of any other curses against you. The atonement of Jesus Christ is the single universal solution that breaks the "authority" of all other curses over you... which you have the right to embrace and apply in faith as a blood-washed child of God.

But keep in mind, that while Christ performed the work to set you free from such curses, you will need to apply that freedom through prayer, faith and a continued relationship with God. And you'll need to separate yourself from things or sinful behavior that is accursed. This does not suggest that you must earn your salvation through works *(Ephesians 2:8-9)*, or return to life under the old law to justify salvation *(Galatians 5:2-4)*. However, while God forgives the sinner, He continues to detest the sin, and requires believers to turn away from wicked and abominable behavior, as described in both the old and new testaments.

For instance, Deuteronomy 27 specifically outlines sinful behavior that is accursed... such as to make a carved or molded image to worship; to treat his father or his mother with contempt; to move his neighbor's landmark; to make the blind to wander off the road; to pervert the justice due the stranger, fatherless, or widow; to lie with his father's wife; to lie with any kind of animal; to lie with his sister; to lie with his mother-in-law; to attack his neighbor secretly; to take a bribe to slay an innocent person; or to not confirm all the words of this law *(Deuteronomy 27:15-26)*.

When a person comes to Christ and repents, God forgives the sinner and nullifies the curse of these sinful acts. But for a believer to continue practicing such things, can welcome their control and evil effects back into their life. The redemption of Jesus breaks the curse of sin over us, but we then must separate ourselves and no longer participate with such cursed things. For example, you may remember the instance of the adulterous woman who was caught and brought to Jesus. He forgave her, but also said to *"go and sin no more" (John 8:10-11)*. To be forgiven of adultery, and yet to continue its practice, is not acceptable.

God forgives the sinner, but sin remains unacceptable and accursed, and the forgiven believer must turn away from this kind of behavior and lifestyle. This includes such perversions as described in Leviticus 18:1–30, or New Testament references to works (sins) of the flesh, described by the Apostle Paul. *"The works of the flesh are evident, which are: adultery, fornication, uncleanness, lewdness, idolatry, sorcery, hatred, contentions, jealousies, outbursts of wrath, selfish ambitions, dissensions, heresies, envy, murders, drunkenness, revelries, and the like; of which I tell you beforehand, just as I also told you in time past, that those who practice such things will not inherit the kingdom of God" (Galatians 5:19-21).*

Many have asked about "generational curses," such as a father's sins passed on to his children and subsequent grandchildren, such as this scripture alludes to, *"...visiting the iniquity of the fathers on the children to the third and fourth generation" (Numbers 14:18). (See Exodus 20:5, Deuteronomy 5:9)* This does not mean that a child must pay for the sins of their father *(Ezekiel 18:20)* ... but it means that the sinful behavior of fathers, grandfathers, great-grandfathers is often replicated by their offspring. This largely due to a child's nature to imitate the same sins and mistakes they witness by their fathers, but can also become associated with evil spirits who attempt to perpetuate or pass-down flawed family traits from one generation to the next.

As I've stated, when a father receives the redemption of Jesus Christ, a continued cycle of such curses or devilish exploits can cease... as long as the father also repents (turns away and ceases) from a lifestyle of sinful, cursed behavior. If repentant fathers discover that their children are following their old sinful patterns, they should sit down with their child, confess their sins and faults of the past, and pray with them to break any spirit influences or continued patterns of such sinful behavior.

So what about spells, curses or hexes that come from persons in the occult or who practice sorcery?
If you are a follower of Christ, walking close with Him through prayer and His Word, and are living a Godly lifestyle... any attempts to cast spells or curses on you should have no effect. The Bible says, *"Like a fluttering sparrow or a darting swallow, an undeserved curse will not land on its intended victim" (Proverbs 26:2 NLT).* This means that a curse cannot stick against someone who is forgiven and who has turned away from cursed-associations from their life. And as we have shared, such acts of sorcery and the occult originate with Satan... over whom you have victory and authority, through the greater power of Christ's indwelling Spirit in you. *"He who is in you is greater than he who is in the world" (1 John 4:4).*

However, if you find yourself in a situation that you suspect that you are dealing with the effects of sorcery, such as a spell or curse, you should take the same action that any believer should when under attack by the devil. Pull yourself close to the Lord and His strength *(James 4:7-8),* and utilize the spiritual weaponry He provides for you to use against the enemy *(Ephesians 6:10-18).*

Even if you are aware of "persons" involved with sorcery or the occult, who may be instigating such things, remember again that your conflict is "not" with "human beings" *(Ephesians 6:12),* but with wicked spiritual entities which must be overcome by spiritual means. *"For the weapons of our warfare are not carnal but mighty in God for pulling down strongholds" (2 Corinthians 10:3-4).*

49. Can Prayer Protect Me From "Hauntings?"

Over years of ministry, I found that most concerns about such things originate from superstitions, over-active imaginations or from other factors such as watching horror films or the use of stimulants. However, I have also ministered to those who have had credible encounters with ghostly visitations, which have always turned out to be manifestations of demon spirits, often masquerading as deceased personalities. In such instances, spirits generally depart and cease their harassments when a believer prays and demands such things to depart in Jesus' name.

Such spirits usually seem to associate with, or follow people who have entertained their activity in some way Perhaps they dabbled with paranormal interests, or participated with or consulted occult practitioners, such as clairvoyants, psychics, witches or spiritualists (something that is extremely dangerous and condemned by scripture *Deuteronomy 18:10-12*). Others may have been the unwitting victims of black magic, spells, or other occultic practices.

But there are also instances in which spirits seem to remain associated with a place, such as we might think of a "haunted house." While I can only speculate how such alleged "hauntings" begin, it appears that after a demonized person dies, such displaced spirits "may" possibly remain or "roam" the place or territory where their past activity was especially affluent, such as the "dry places" described in Luke 11:24. Regardless whether this theory has merit, I have indeed ministered to persons who have been troubled by such things, and can attest that the authority in the name of Jesus, will expel "spooks" as effectively as demons... which I believe are one in the same.

Several years ago, I encountered one such instance connected with the home of a military family who had begun attending our church. Teresa, a Marine Sargent's wife and mother of three young teens, came to see me about strange occurrences in their new home. The family had been transferred from another base in recent months, and while her husband was still away on deployment she and her kids had settled into their on-base townhouse. However, shortly after their arrival, they started finding things moved around the house without explanation. Doors were found opened that had been closed, doors were also discovered closed, that had been previously open.

Concerned that a prowler might be entering the home with a previous tenant's key, I advised her to change the locks and call the police. I prayed with her about these and other spiritual matters, and assumed the issue would be resolved... but it was not.

A couple weeks later, she returned with more reports of strange happenings. Even with doors solidly locked, she and her children continued witnessing similar patterns. One night they were surprised to hear and see someone walking past a hallway, but when they investigated, no one could be found.

Had it been only this mother's observations, it would have been easier to dismiss these spooky notions as if her mind was playing tricks, hallucinations or the like. But her kids affirmed that they saw these things too. And according to what they said, they had never seen or experienced anything like this before moving to the Navy base housing.

Finally, after several more days, both the mother and kids came to see me again, explaining that the matter had erupted into something much worse. They explained that they all had started seeing a person or "being" walking through the house, carrying a candle and dressed in a hooded black cape. This was quite alarming and rose far above mysterious sounds or misplaced objects. They saw this being on several occasions, and as before, couldn't find a trace of this person or entity, when they later tried to find them.

But to make the matter more disturbing, her husband returned briefly from his duty abroad, and saw the being too. At first, he laughed-off their stories about ghosts, only as wild imagination, until one night. Both Teresa and her husband were asleep in bed when they were startled awake by someone else in the room. They sat up, and to their horror, in the dim light both could see a black-robed being standing at the foot of the bed. It then turned, walked out and disappeared! Her husband completely freaked out. He had no idea what to do except to move away if possible, but before he could make that happen, he was called out again on deployment. Teresa and her kids found themselves alone again for weeks, frightened by what was happening, and didn't want to return to the house.

At this point, I deduced what the issue was. I explained that these apparitions were likely demonic manifestations that needed expelled from the home, or from whatever ties they might have with their lives. I further added that to keep these things away, she along with her kids and husband needed to give their lives fully to Christ, to fill their home with prayer and devotion to Jesus, so such things wouldn't return. After sharing these things, the mom prayed to rededicate her life to Christ, and all three kids prayed for Jesus to come into their heart too.

After this, confident that everyone now had Christ's Spirit in their hearts, we all headed over to their townhouse to conduct a prayer meeting. For a couple hours or more, I read from scripture, led in worship and songs with the family, and commanded the demon spirits to depart the home by the authority of Jesus name. Then after prayer, we went through the home with anointing oil (a symbol of the Holy Spirit), and I dabbed a spot on each doorway, praying and claiming the home as a refuge of Christ's peace and safety. When it was over, we all felt the peace of Jesus in the townhouse, and I believed that as long as they followed-through with their commitment to Christ, they would never be bothered again.

As a result, the family never reported any more occurrences of apparitions. I never knew for sure what brought this on to begin with, but it could have been connected to something that the family brought with them, such as a previous association with the occult, or a spell directed toward them from an occultist. Or it could have been associated with some kind of occultic or satanic activity that took place there previously. I have no idea... but I do know that Jesus is always the answer, even for a haunted townhouse on a Navy base.

As I've repeated several times in this writing, resisting the devil always involves drawing closer to God and submitting yourself to Him. This is the foundation of all spiritual warfare. As scripture says, *"Submit yourself to*

God. Resist the devil and he will flee from you. Draw near to God and He will draw near to you" (James 4:7-8).

Please note, however, that James describes this as something a believer must take the initiative to do. Obviously, the Holy Spirit is always at work, drawing you toward the Lord *(John 6:44)*, but no one can submit yourself to God, except you. And when you reach out to pull yourself toward Him, He will draw near to you.

(For a detailed description of how to resist the devil, go back and read Question 42, *"Can Prayer Make the Devil Leave Me Alone?"*)

50. How Do We Know Healing is God's Will?

We know it's God will to heal for a lot of reasons, beginning with its inseparable relationship from salvation, as we described. God not only wants all mankind to be saved *(2 Peter 3:9)*, but to receive all the benefits, including healing, paid for by the redemption of Jesus Christ.

If this were not true, then we should find at least a few instances in the Gospels where Jesus declined or turned persons away for healing... but we find none. There are eleven recorded instances that persons approached Jesus for healing, and never once did He turn anyone away or state that it was not His will. In fact, in one instance, a leper specifically asked whether it was His will. He inquired, *"Lord, if it is your will you can heal me."* And what was His response? *"Jesus extended his hand and said, it's my will; Be healed! And the man's leprosy vanished" (Matthew 8:2-3).*

Not only did Jesus not refuse healing to anyone during His earthly ministry, but the scriptures say that Jesus went about *"...healing ALL who were oppressed by the devil..." (Acts 10:38)*. It also says, He went to the villages and towns... *"healing every sickness and every disease among the people" (Matthew 9:35)*.

Another powerful reason we know God wants to heal is because of the name with which He identifies himself in the Old Testament. In many instances He extended His name to describe His provisions, such as He did after the Israelites crossed the Red Sea. He promised Moses and the people that if they would be faithful and obey His commands, He would protect them from disease, explaining that His name is *"JEHOVAH RAPHA,"* or *"I am the LORD that heals you" (Exodus 15:26)*. How could God reveal His will more clearly, than to give himself a name that says He heals you? Not only is it His will, it's His name... it's who He is and what He does.

And here's something else to consider. Several years ago, I heard a doctor give an interesting talk about the body's amazing healing abilities. He described how that physicians readily acknowledge that medicine has no healing powers of its own, but can only help patients by coordinating with the body's natural healing properties.

For instance, from the moment someone gets a cut on their foot or hand, the immune system goes to work, fighting infection to heal itself. He explained that healing is not an unusual event that only happens occasionally, but is the body's most common response to injury and illness, a product of divine engineering in every human being.

So, if our Creator designed healing to be the body's natural normal response to illness and injury, what does that tell us about His willingness to Heal? Our body bears witness that healing is the normal pattern, something God wants and desires... the reason He placed it in our physiology.

Furthermore, think about this. If it's not God's will to heal you, what sense would it make to go to the doctor? Can he overrule the will of God? And for that matter, if it's God's will for you to remain sick, wouldn't it be a defiant act against His will, for you to go to the doctor?

Thank the Lord for wonderful physicians who understand God's role in the body's natural healing virtues, and for those who also pray for God to add His supernatural health and healing to their patients.

51. How to Receive Healing from God

Healing is an integral part of the gospel message, a benefit of salvation that is as accessible as the forgiveness of sins. However, it appears that God may bring healing to you from a variety or combination of ways... such as through the prayers of yourself or others *(Mark 11:24)*, the prayer of faith and laying on of hands by elders or ministers *(Mark 16:17, James 5:14-15)*, or by the manifestation of spiritual gifts, such as the *"gifts of healing" or "working of miracles" (1 Corinthians 12:9-10)*.

Regardless of the means God may use, here are five steps to get started in seeking the Lord's healing:

(1) Submit yourself to God – As much as it is God's will and desire to heal, such things as unconfessed sin, disobedience, unbelief, or unforgiveness toward others can

194

hinder your reception of healing, and in some instances, could actually be part of the original cause of your illness. Any affliction should be a time for self-examination, to come before the Lord in humility, surrendering yourself and drawing near to Him. James wrote, *"Therefore submit to God. Resist the devil and he will flee from you. Draw near to God and He will draw near to you. Cleanse your hands, you sinners; and purify your hearts, you double-minded. Lament and mourn and weep! Let your laughter be turned to mourning and your joy to gloom. Humble yourselves in the sight of the Lord, and He will lift you up"* (James 4:7-10).

One of the most common moments that people attest to divine healing, is during their participation with the Lord's Supper (Holy Communion). This is largely because receiving the bread and juice, symbols of Christ's bodily sufferings, helps amplify their faith in the atoning sufferings of Christ, which He gave for our redemption and healing. *"He personally carried our sins in his body on the cross so that we can be dead to sin and live for what is right. By his wounds you are healed"* (1 Peter 2:24 NLT).

(2) Look to God's Word – Read and meditate continuously upon the healing promises in the Bible. As you let them absorb into your inner man, it will bring a great sense of assurance. This is the confidence of faith that comes as you open your heart to the Word of God (Romans 10:17). *"My son, give attention to my words; incline your ear to my sayings. Do not let them depart from your eyes; keep them in the midst of your heart; For they are life to those who find them, and health to all their flesh"* (Proverbs 4:20-22). How important it is that we focus upon God's Word, as this is the source of His healing power. *"He sent His word and healed them, And delivered them from their destructions" (Psalms 107:20).*

(3) Pray in Faith – Place your faith in the finished work of Christ's sufferings in behalf of your sickness or disease. Christ has already paid for your healing and has placed it into effect, making it available to you. Now it's up to you to accept His finished work by faith. *"Therefore I say to you, whatever things you ask when you pray, believe that you receive them, and you will have them" (Mark 11:24).* Keep standing on His healing promises by faith, and declare them aloud, giving God praise and thanks. God will be faithful to His Word, if you will be faithful to believe!

(4) Call for Church Elders – Request for the elders or ministers of the church to anoint you with oil and pray the prayer of faith over you. The Bible says, *"Is anyone among you sick? Let him call for the elders of the church, and let them pray over him, anointing him with oil in the name of the Lord. And the prayer of faith will save the sick, and the Lord will raise him up. And if he has committed sins, he will be forgiven" (James 5:14-15).*

Notice that it says the prayer of faith *"shall save the sick."* The oil has no mystical powers in itself, but is simply a symbol of the Holy Spirit. Ask the elders and other believers to lay hands on you and pray. As the scripture says, *"...they will lay hands on the sick..."* and notice, it says that *"they will recover" (Mark 16:18).*

(5) Keep Believing – Don't stop praying and believing. This is the most common reason why people don't receive healing. They get discouraged and give up their faith. Most would prefer to receive instantaneous healing (which

196

is a manifestation of spiritual gifts, *1 Corinthians 12:9-10)*, but most healings occur gradually over time. Be patient and be steadfast in your faith. Keep embracing and declaring His promises of healing, thanking and praising Him for bringing it to pass. *"...Do not become sluggish, but imitate those who through faith and patience inherit the promises" (Hebrews 6:12).*

52. Why Should I Bother God With My Prayers?

It doesn't bother Him. It might seem that God has his hands full with a lot of other things, like dealing with several billion other people. However the amazing thing, is that He has no limitations, and can be everywhere at once, hearing and answering each one's prayers simultaneously.

Be assured, the Lord is as interested in you as anything or anyone else. And He has such detailed knowledge of you and your needs, that the He even knows the number of hairs on your head *(Matthew 10:30)*. Everywhere we look in scripture, we find His encouragements to come to Him with our needs. He alone has the answer for every problem. *"Let us therefore come boldly to the throne of grace, that we may obtain mercy and find grace to help in time of need" (Hebrews 4:16).*

Jesus also repeatedly encouraged His followers to bring their concerns to the Lord. And He promised that the Father would be gracious to each one who bring their needs to Him. *"Ask, and it will be given to you; seek, and you will find; knock, and it will be opened to you. For everyone who asks receives, and he who seeks finds, and to him who knocks it will be opened. Or what man is there among you who, if his son asks for bread, will give him a stone? Or if he asks for a fish, will he give him a serpent? If you then, being evil, know how to give good gifts to your children, how much more will your Father who is in heaven give good things to those who ask Him!" (Matthew 7:7-11).*

Does this sound like a God who would be bothered by your prayers? Obviously, not. He cares about you and desires your fellowship in prayer, and wants you to bring your needs and concerns to Him. *"Cast all your care upon Him, for He cares for you" (1 Peter 5:7).*

The Christian author, Max Lucado said, *"Prayer is not a privilege just for the pious or an opportunity for a chosen few. Prayer is God's open invitation to talk: simply, openly and powerfully."[1]*

[1] *Before Amen: The Power of a Simple Prayer, Max Lucado, 2014*

53. Can Prayer Bring Me a Boyfriend or Girlfriend?

Sure. God cares about every aspect of our life, including our need for friendship and companionship. But again, as with anything we ask God for, our requests must come into harmony with His wishes, and must fit into His Holy standards. In other words, your prayer for a boyfriend or girlfriend should be based on the motive of wholesome, Christian friendship or for marriage, not to fulfill your lusts or to fornicate.

Sexual companionship is certainly a normal, legitimate desire that God cares about as well, but His plan for that involves marriage between one person of the opposite sex. When our heart and motives are surrendered to God and

His will, He certainly will hear our prayers regarding these matters... and will bring the right husband or wife into our life.

With regard to marriage companionship, Jesus said *"But from the beginning of the creation, God made them male and female. For this reason a man shall leave his father and mother and be joined to his wife, and the two shall become one flesh; so then they are no longer two, but one flesh. Therefore what God has joined together, let not man separate"* (Mark 10:6-9).

The Apostle Paul also wrote, *"Marriage is honorable among all, and the bed undefiled; but fornicators and adulterers God will judge"* (Hebrews 13:4). *(See also Galatians 5:19, Ephesians 5:3, Colossians 3:5)*

54. Can Prayer Make Someone Fall in Love with Me?

No. You can certainly ask the Lord to bring a special person into your life for Godly companionship or marriage (as shared previously), but this will be based on the Lord's will and guidance for both of your lives. God will not make anyone to do anything against their will, and prayer cannot be used to manipulate, control or coerce anyone to do something for your purposes.

As another way to understand this, let consider the idea of praying for persons to get saved. This is certainly a request that God is pleased with... but again, He will not force anyone do anything against their will. He will beckon to their heart by His Holy Spirit, inviting them to come to Him... but it's up to them to respond, to make that decision. *"Behold, I stand at the door and knock. If*

*anyone hears My voice and opens the door, I will come in
to him and dine with him, and he with Me" (Revelation
3:20).*

Trying to control or manipulate people is more closely
associated with witchcraft, which often attempts to do so
with the use of spells, incantations, mysticism, etc.
Witchcraft has its origin with Satan, the archenemy of
God, who opposes the followers of Jesus Christ.

With regard to a companion, you will do better to simply
pray and trust the Lord to guide you to the right husband
or wife. The psalmist said, *"Trust in the Lord with all your
heart, And lean not on your own understanding; In all
your ways acknowledge Him, And He shall direct your
paths" (Proverbs 3:5-6).*

55. Can Prayer Help Get Me a Job?

Absolutely. As we've already shared, God wants every
able-bodied person to work. Paul said, *"Never be lazy, but
work hard and serve the Lord enthusiastically" (Romans
12:11 NLT).* The Psalmist also warned against laziness,
saying *"Despite their desires, the lazy will come to ruin, for
their hands refuse to work" (Proverbs 21:25 NLT).*

The Lord desires His people to be industrious and to be
blessed in their labors. If we will continue to pray and
seek His guidance, He can connect us with the right kind
of career, employment or business that will fit our
personality, interests and skills. As the psalmist wrote,
*"For You are my rock and my fortress; Therefore, for Your
name's sake, Lead me and guide me" (Psalms 31:3). (Also
Proverbs 3:5-6).*

When God answers such a prayer, He also expects us to be ready to give our best and perform an honest day's labor for our employer, not to be slothful, unreliable or dishonest. *"Whatever your hand finds to do, do it with your might" (Ecclesiastes 9:10).* He wants his people to have good work ethics... that is, to be diligent, hard-working, honest, and dependable. He will bless the diligent worker with prosperousness. *"Lazy people are soon poor; hard workers get rich" (Proverbs 10:4 NLT).*

The Lord will also want you to honor Him with the principle of tithing... that is, giving Him the first 10% of your increase... which He claims as His own *(Malachi 3:8-9).* Tithing is an expression of thanksgiving and faith in God that dates back to the days of Abraham, and denotes your trust in Him as your provider and the Lord over all things. God promises to meet the needs of the tither, and to rebuke the devourer of your blessings. *"Bring all the tithes into the storehouse, That there may be food in My house, And try Me now in this, Says the Lord of hosts, If I will not open for you the windows of heaven And pour out for you such blessing That there will not be room enough to receive it. And I will rebuke the devourer for your sakes, So that he will not destroy the fruit of your ground, Nor shall the vine fail to bear fruit for you in the field, Says the Lord of hosts" (Malachi 3:10-11).*

56. Can Prayer Help Supply My Financial Needs?

Yes, God cares about your daily necessities of life... food, clothing, shelter. He promises to provide these and add many other blessings, if you will pray and ask Him "as you also" follow Him with your life. **To obtain God's**

help in meeting your financial and material needs, here are five principles to apply:

(1) Seek Him First – Jesus gave a very simple explanation of how to obtain God's help in meeting your needs. From His sermon on the mount, He said, *"Therefore do not worry, saying, What shall we eat? or What shall we drink? or What shall we wear? For after all these things the Gentiles seek. For your heavenly Father knows that you need all these things. But <u>seek first the kingdom of God and His righteousness</u>, and all these things shall be added to you." (Matthew 6:31-33).*

When followers of Christ have needs, they don't have to share the same sense of worry or despair as the unbelieving world. Jesus explained that those who put their faith in God, and who will look to Him and His values as their highest priorities, the Lord will make sure that their needs are "added" to their life.

To "seek first His kingdom and righteousness," means to make it our highest goal to pursue a relationship with God... to seek after His spiritual values, to reach toward a lifestyle of obedience and faithfulness to those things that please Him. This kind of person makes Jesus the Lord (boss) of their life, with the objective of honoring Him in everything they do or say. And if they make mistakes, they repent of their sins, get back up and continue walking with the Lord.

Such followers of the Lord will often see added provisions and blessings to their life even before they ask... and when they pray and ask God for His help, He will assuredly respond and bless them. As David stated in his psalm, *"I have been young, and now am old; Yet I have not seen the*

righteous forsaken, Nor his descendants begging bread"
(Psalms 37:25).

(2) Work diligently – Even though the Lord promises to
meet your needs, this doesn't mean that He exempts us
from toil or labor. The Lord expects all able-bodied
persons to work *(2 Thessalonians 3:10)*, and expects us to
perform our tasks with diligence and excellence *"Whatever
your hand finds to do, do it with your might..."*
(Ecclesiastes 9:10).

The Lord blesses strong work ethics, and will bless the
fruit of our labors so we can provide for our family. *"How
joyful are those who fear the Lord — all who follow his
ways! You will enjoy the fruit of your labor. How joyful
and prosperous you will be!" (Psalms 128:1-2 NLT).*

But how can God's work ethics be honored if you don't
have a job? While you are praying and seeking
employment, give yourself to volunteering at the church,
or performing acts of kindness, or giving assistance to the
needy. When I was out of a job for a time years ago, the
Lord put it on my heart to give my available time to Him,
as though He was my employer. I went down to the
church and did whatever they needed done... dug ditches,
cleaned up the grounds, did chores and odd jobs.

I did this, not expecting anything back from the church...
but as an expression of my faith in God, for Him to meet
my needs. And whad'ya know, at the end of those weeks, I
received an unexpected check from our insurance
company, a significant refund for premiums I overpaid in
the past! PTL! The amount was just enough to pay our
bills. Some might call this a just lucky break, but these
"divine coincidences" are often the way God works. Over

the years, I've seen the Lord do similar kinds of things over and over... finding ways to answer my prayers and meet our needs.

The basic message here is, even if you are temporarily without an earthly employer, God still blesses the principle of hard work. Until you find employment, look to Him as your employer... give your time and labor to Him. And even after you have a job, keep looking to Him as the one you are working for, the real source of your provisions and needs.

One of the great truths of scripture is to realize that the Lord, not man, is our provider. As a matter of fact, one of the names used for God in the Old Testament (*Jehovah-jireh*, in the King James Bible, but more accurately pronounced *Yahweh-yir´eh*), means the *"Lord Who Provides" (Genesis 22:13-14)*. And if you look to Him as your provider, and honor Him in faith and obedience, He will do exactly that! *"Even strong young lions sometimes go hungry, but those who trust in the Lord will lack no good thing." (Psalms 34:10 NLT)*.

(3) Honor Him with Your Firstfruits – Honoring the Lord with the first-fruits of our increase is another important aspect to putting Christ first in our lives. *"Honor the Lord with your possessions, And with the firstfruits of all your increase" (Proverbs 3:9)*. This is also referred to as the tithe, or the first 10% of our income. God promises to pour out blessing to those who honor Him in this principle *"Bring all the tithes into the storehouse, That there may be food in My house, And try Me now in this," Says the Lord of hosts, "If I will not open for you the windows of heaven And pour out for you such*

blessing That there will not be room enough to receive it"
(Malachi 3:10).

The Lord also promises to bring abundant blessings back
to those who give offerings or gifts in His name. *"Give,*
and you will receive. Your gift will return to you in full—
pressed down, shaken together to make room for more,
running over, and poured into your lap. The amount you
give will determine the amount you get back" (Luke 6:38
NLT).

Giving to the church, the Lord's work, and to such things
as world evangelism is vitally important. But as God
prospers us, He also looks for us to use our blessings to
help those who are less fortunate, and promises to prosper
those who are generous to help the poor. *"Whoever gives to*
the poor will lack nothing, but those who close their eyes to
poverty will be cursed" (Proverbs 28:27 NLT). If fact, the
scriptures say that when you help the poor, you lend to
the Lord... who will repay you. *"If you help the poor, you*
are lending to the Lord— and he will repay you!"
(Proverbs 19:17 NLT).

(4) Be a Good Steward – It is also important to be a
good steward of what God gives you. Stewardship basically
refers to the efficient management of resources, and since
everything you have comes from God, He wants you to use
what He gives you wisely. This means that He wants you
to be faithful in giving to His work, contributing to the
needs of the poor... but also wants you to be prudent with
how you use all your resources. He wants you to live
frugally within your means *(Luke 14:28-29,* not to be
wasteful, or to get caught up in reckless spending or debt
that can end up owning you. *"The wicked borrow and*

205

never repay, but the godly are generous givers" (Psalms
37:21 NLT).

This is important to remember. Regardless of how much
God blesses a person, it's always possible to outspend the
blessings of God. On many occasions, I've seen people
come into wealth, perhaps from an inheritance or such,
only to watch them quickly squander it away, then have to
struggle for survival again. This kind of careless attitude
with money will likely guarantee a person's continued
state of poverty, regardless of how much money they earn
or receive.

The Lord can meet our needs by a variety of ways... but
He often does so by blessing and stretching your basic
earnings or adding to what you already have, like the
miracle of the fish and loaves *(Matthew 14:13-21)*. If you
honor Him and His principles as we've described above,
He will make sure that your dollar goes farther... and
you'll be surprised by the discounts, deals, bonuses and
refunds that come your way. *"A faithful man will abound
with blessings..."* (Proverbs 28:20).

If you make mistakes with the way you handle money, ask
His forgiveness and start over with the principles we've
shared here. Fortunately, God is gracious and redemptive,
and always willing to help those who repent of and learn
from their mistakes.

(5) Pray in Faith – Whenever a person's life pleases the
Lord, he can be assured that the Lord will hear and
answer his prayers to meet his needs. *"And whatever we
ask we receive from Him, because we keep His
commandments and do those things that are pleasing in
His sight"* (1 John 3:22).

God can meet our needs in any variety of ways. He can provide a job, and bless our labors with increase, or He may send blessing from an entirely unexpected source. This is how He provided for George Muller's orphanage ministry, generations ago in Bristol, England. Muller was an astonishing man of prayer and faith, who fed and educated multitudes of children, without any other support than prayer. He operated his ministry entirely by faith, standing solely on God's promises, as described by the Apostle Paul, *"And my God shall supply all your need according to His riches in glory by Christ Jesus"* *(Philippians 4:19).*

In one instance, a day came that Muller's orphanage had run entirely out of food. As mealtime approached, Muller assembled his three-hundred children before empty plates at the dining tables. He led them in prayer, thanking God in faith for the food he believed the Lord would provide. And within moments came a knock at the door from a baker, who had surplus loaves of bread he wanted to donate. And after that, a milkman dropped by with gallons of fresh milk to contribute. This miracle of God's provision was typical to the daily ministry of George Muller, who during his life, fed and cared for more than 10,000 orphans, raising up 117 schools and providing Christian education for over 120,000 children.

Follow the patterns and principles that we've described here, and if provision doesn't come immediately, keep praying and trusting God until it does. God is faithful, His Word is true, and He will honor the prayer of faith in the name of Jesus.

"Keep on asking, and you will receive what you ask for. Keep on seeking, and you will find. Keep on knocking, and

the door will be opened to you. For everyone who asks, receives. Everyone who seeks, finds. And to everyone who knocks, the door will be opened. "You parents—if your children ask for a loaf of bread, do you give them a stone instead? Or if they ask for a fish, do you give them a snake? Of course not! So if you sinful people know how to give good gifts to your children, how much more will your heavenly Father give good gifts to those who ask him" (Matthew 7:7-11 NLT).

My Experiences with Miraculous Provisions

From my early childhood in Sunday School, I can remember hearing these encouraging promises from the scriptures, even the flannelgraph illustrations that were used, showing Jesus feeding the little birds or giving colorful blossoms to the lilies of the field *(Matthew 6:26-28)*. However, as I grew up, I always assumed these lessons had only been metaphors. I could hardly imagine a situation that I would need supernatural provision... until I came to Christ and was called to serve in ministry.

After our first year of marriage, my wife and I felt the Lord leading us toward full-time evangelism, and linked up with a college ministry that sent couples on mission trips to a variety of campuses around the country. However, after quitting our jobs and venturing about a thousand miles from home, we were surprised to learn that this well-intentioned, but poorly-organized ministry provided little in the way of financial support.

It was a shock to learn that we were pretty much on our own. But believing that God had led us down this path, we chose to continue on for the short-term... relying only on God to provide for us. And as it turns out, this is what

God really had in mind all along, as He used this experience to teach us how to trust Him to meet our needs.

I had personally never been through anything like this... so far from home, with little money or resources. Not even friends or family to turn to if necessary. But we pressed forward, pulling a small camper behind our car... and amazingly, as we prayed and stood on the promises of His Word, He never failed us. One promise we frequently quoted, was from an epistle of Paul, *"And my God shall supply all your need according to His riches in glory by Christ Jesus" (Philippians 4:19).*

We nearly ran out of money or provisions on many occasions, but somehow God always met our need. In some instances, strangers just walked up and just handed us money, even in cities I'd never visited before. And while not usually scheduled to speak anywhere on Sundays, we would always visit the local churches, where we'd often be asked to share or preach... which would bring about free-will offerings that helped meet our need.

Of course, we were not without very trying moments, such as during our visit to Syracuse University. By the end of our week spent there, our money and resources were drained. I had less than five dollars, with a near empty gas tank. As my wife and I returned to our little camper that Friday night, I felt discouraged and ready to give up, but we knelt and prayed throughout the evening until we fell asleep.

The next thing I remember was awaking to a knocking at the trailer door. The sun was just coming up, and there was fresh dusting of snow on the ground outside. Since we knew no one there, I opened the door cautiously... and standing there was a short fellow with a grin, holding several grocery bags. *"Here, these are for you,"* he said, as he turned and scampered away on the snowy sidewalk.

Barely awake, my wife and I were shocked by the stranger's brief visit. And as we looked through the sacks, we found groceries and other items, even many of our preferred brands. And in the bottom of one sack, was an envelope of cash, just enough to fill the gas tank. No one else knew our need or how much we needed a miracle, except our Lord. Before doing anything else that morning, we spent time thanking and praising God for hearing our prayers, and for meeting our needs again, as He did time and again.

57. Can Prayer Cause Me to Become Rich?

God can, and sometimes does bring great wealth to some, especially to those whom He sees will be faithful to use such resources in Godly ways... to advance God's Kingdom, to help the needy or to reach souls for Christ. HOWEVER, for many people, money is too much of a temptation, a pitfall that often leads to all kinds of other problems. *"For the love of money is a root of all kinds of evil, for which some have strayed from the faith in their greediness, and pierced themselves through with many sorrows" (1 Timothy 6:10).* For this and other reasons, the Lord will not always grant such prayers for great wealth.

Unfortunately, if God made everyone rich, many if not most would forget about Him and fill their life with other things. The Lord loves you and wants you to serve Him and go to Heaven, far more than He wants you to be rich.

"For what profit is it to a man if he gains the whole world, and loses his own soul? Or what will a man give in exchange for his soul?" (Matthew 16:26).

However, God definitively does care about the needs of you and your family, and will certainly answer your prayers for such necessities of life. In fact, the Bible has a lot to say about this, such as in Jesus' sermon on the mount, where He described how the Father clothes and feeds all the creatures of His creation *(Matthew 6:24-33)*. He said, *"...Therefore do not worry, saying, 'What shall we eat?' or 'What shall we drink?' or 'What shall we wear?' For after all these things the Gentiles seek. For your heavenly Father knows that you need all these things. But* seek first the kingdom of God *and* His righteousness, *and all* these things shall be added *to you" (Matthew 6:31-33).*

Jesus explained that the Father's method of providing for His people, was not for them to focus their lives on "things" such as money or material matters. This kind of appetite can dominate and hinder one's relationship to Him *(Matthew 6:24)*. But rather, He admonished that they should focus their primary attention on pursuing the ideals of God's kingdom and His righteousness.By seeking first to live for the Lord, to uphold matters of His kingdom and righteousness as their highest priority, the Father assures that their needs and provisions will be "added" to their lives. As the New Living Translation puts it, *"Seek the Kingdom of God above all else, and live righteously, and he will give you everything you need" (Matthew 6:33 NLT)*.

Although many pastors and ministers do a great job teaching sound principles of Biblical stewardship and divine blessing, there's also a variety of controversial teachers who promote ideas that all Christians should be rich. While there are aspects of Biblical truth in such teachings, it's an exaggeration to teach that material wealth is promised to all believers.

Most generally, when God blesses persons with wealth, it is due to a combination of things. The wisdom and diligence He bestows for such persons to handle finances, along with their persistence to put the Lord first with their lives *(Matthew 6:33)*. The Lord will always bless those who honor Him with their tithes, their offerings, and their generosity toward the needs of others *(Malachi 3:10)*. Solomon said, *"The generous will prosper; those who refresh others will themselves be refreshed" (Proverbs 11:25 NLT)*.

In many cases, God has "already" blessed his people with abundance... but they've sometimes been poor stewards of His blessings. Unfortunately, many people routinely "outspend the blessings of God." For instance, I've seen God do astounding things for people at times... such as to bless them with miraculous sums of money, only to see them to either squander or overspend it. Just imagine, to be blessed with a million dollars, only to spend it all... and then go into debt and spend another million more. I've seen this sort of thing happen over and over with people.

"Counting the cost" or "budgeting" is a good Biblical principle that Christians should practice with the blessings that God provides. *"For which of you, intending to build a tower, does not sit down first and count the cost, whether he has enough to finish it" (Luke 14:28)*.

58. Can God Talk to Us When We Pray to Him?

Yes, as we have shared previously, prayer can be considered a "two way" form of communication, that when we talk to Him, He will often also speak to us through His Holy Spirit. Andrew Murray, the late missionary and intercessor, said, *"Prayer is not monologue, but dialogue. God's voice in response to mine is its most essential part."*[1]

There are numerous examples in the Old Testament, but also in the New... as shown in this instance of the early church. After praying and fasting, the Lord spoke to church leaders to dedicate Barnabas and Saul for a special mission. *"As they ministered to the Lord and fasted, the Holy Spirit said, Now separate to Me Barnabas and Saul for the work to which I have called them" (Acts 13:2).*

Perhaps the most common way God speaks to believers is as they meditate on His written Word, the Bible. The Holy Spirit will often amplify the impact of particular passages, bringing our attention to thoughts or truths that He especially wants to impress on us. At other times, we may sense the Holy Spirit communicating with us as we pray, or as we're simply thinking about the Lord.

God seems to speak to different people in a variety of ways. Some may claim to hear God's audible voice, while others may hear what is often described as the "still small voice," or perhaps an inner awareness, assurance or leading. Others even receive communication through dreams or visions. But the most important thing to remember is that the Lord will never say anything that contradicts His written Word. If we feel that God has

213

spoken to us about a matter, we should always validate it with the scripture. And if we can confirm that He is genuinely speaking with us, we'd best pay attention... believe, obey or respond what He has to say. He obviously doesn't communicate with us without a reason.

Both my wife and I have heard from the Lord in a variety of ways over the years, but one particular incident in 1981 took us both by surprise. During the second week of March, we were in the third month of our first pastorate near Chicago... and my wife was pregnant, still about six weeks away from the birth of our daughter. One morning, she shared a disturbing dream she had the night before, that newly elected president, Ronald Reagan, had been shot.

I was surprised, as I wasn't aware of any dark dreams she'd ever had like this before. But I just shrugged it off, thinking it was maybe just a goofy dream that any of us might experience. However, two weeks later, on the afternoon of March 30, I was listening to the radio while working outside the church, when I heard the shocking news. President Reagan had been shot by an attempted assassin... not killed, but seriously wounded!

I was stunned, realizing my wife's dream had not just been a strange coincidence. She had received an advance warning from God. But we were both perplexed, wondering why the Lord might reveal such a thing to persons so far away, without any means to warn the president. However, learning later that others had similar advanced revelations about the shooting, we realized that God was warning many of His people to "pray" for the president. As a young pastor, I should have had the insight to lead our congregation in prayer for our nation's leader, but was too ignorant to perceive this as something originating from God.

Since that time, if we have a premonition or dream about anyone, we take no chances and we pray for them. I have no idea, but perhaps God has used our prayers along with others, to bring unknown blessings... or to even divert what may have been otherwise disastrous.

Of course, not every purported dream, revelation or thought comes from God. Sometimes they may only be adventures whipped up in our own mind. And since Satan can also speak to us in subtle thoughts or suggestions, it is important to be wary, and authenticate any such impressions with God's Word and prayer. For obvious reasons, we must always guard our thoughts by keeping Christ and His Word in the forefront of our life and mind. *"Let the words of my mouth and the meditation of my heart Be acceptable in Your sight, O Lord, my strength and my Redeemer." (Psalms 19:14).*

How to Pray and Hear from God

(1) Pray and ask Him directly – As we have said, His communication will not always come in the form of articulated words, but what might emerge as thoughts, an awareness, discernment, a leading, and so forth. *"Call to Me, and I will answer you..." (Jeremiah 33:3).*

(2) Meditate upon God's Word – God will speak personally to our heart as we read and medicate upon his Word. And how important for us to be grounded in the knowledge of His scriptures, as He never speak anything to us in contradiction to His written Word. *"All Scripture is given by inspiration of God, and is profitable for* *doctrine, for reproof, for correction, for instruction in righteousness" (2 Timothy 3:16).*

(3) Be Prepared to Seek and Wait – Seek the Lord and wait upon Him through prayer and fasting, don't be impatient. *"As they ministered to the Lord and fasted, the Holy Spirit said, Now separate to Me Barnabas and Saul for the work to which I have called them" (Acts 13:2).*

(4) Consecrate Yourself – If you want to hear from the Holy Spirit, remember that He is a "holy spirit," and is more apt to speak through the life of one who is submitted and consecrated to Him. In other words, if a person can't hear God talking to them about their sinful or immoral behavior, it's not likely they can hear Him speaking about other things either. One of the primary tests of a prophet (one who purports to speak in God's behalf) is the fruit of his/her lifestyle. *"You will know them by their fruits" (Matthew 7:16).*

(5) Pray and Empty Yourself – God is eager to answer your prayers when they fit into His desires for you. However, a lot of times, our prayers must first deal with emptying ourselves of our own self-willed agenda. Combining fasting with prayer is something that especially helps this process of humbling or surrendering ourselves to His will. If you recall Jesus' prayer on the eve before His trial and crucifixion, He didn't press His Heavenly Father to deliver Him from the cross, but wanted His Father's will more than His own. He prayed... *"not my will, but thine be done" (Luke 22:42).* James also explained that prayers often go unanswered because of "self-serving" lusts. *"Ye ask, and receive not, because ye ask amiss, that ye may consume it upon your lusts" (James 4:3 KJV).*

(6) Listen but also be Cautious – It's obvious that God does speak to His people in our present day and age, and I certainly encourage all believers to pray, read God's Word, and listen for the Holy Spirit to speak to their heart. But also, be on guard against extremes or exaggerated teachings, that can often confuse persons from understanding the difference between the Lord's voice and one's own imagination.

[1] *Andrew Murray On Prayer, Andrew Murray, 1917*

59. Can Prayer Save My Marriage?

Yes, it is possible... however the catch to remember here, is that marriage involves the will of "two" persons, not just one. The free will is one of the most sacred things that the Lord has given to each of us, and He will not force anyone to do something against their will. We have the freedom to make our own choices, whether to believe in God or not... whether to follow His ways, or to reject them.

In the case of your spouse, you can be assured that when you pray, God will "deal" with the heart of your spouse by His Holy Spirit. He will appeal to his or her heart to follow the Lord's will, but there is no absolute certainty that your spouse will respond or do precisely as God wants, or as you want.

Another thing to consider is that although we know that God wants all marriages to succeed and not to break up, neither does he want a spouse to surrender themselves or their children back into to an abusive or destructive relationship.

Without a doubt, God is gracious and amazing, and can restore and heal even the worst marriages imaginable. Jesus said, *"With men this is impossible, but with God all things are possible" (Matthew 19:26).*

However much depends on whether the hearts of both spouses are willing to allow God to do what is necessary. For instance, if a husband abused his wife or children, was unfaithful and slept around with other women, or spent his paychecks on booze and partying instead of paying the bills for his family... that man would need to repent and vow to never repeat such sinful acts again.

Until such a gentleman would allow God to transform his behavior, it's not likely the Lord would answer prayer to bring a wife back into a mess like that. And it would be foolish for her to trust her life or her children's again with someone who has such a record of sinful and irresponsible behavior. But before doing anything further to end the marriage, the Lord will likely encourage such a wife to wait, to hopefully allow the husband time to get his life back on the right track. And perhaps in time God can restore such a marriage.

60. Can Prayer Help Get My Children Off Drugs?

God certainly hears and answers prayers with regard to our loved-ones, and especially for our children. I can attest that a mom or dad's prayers for their child, can be quite powerful and effective. This is likely related to how much we love them. The more we care about persons, the more fervent and frequent we will pray for them. James said, *"...The effective, fervent prayer of a righteous man avails much" (James 5:16).*

This lends strong support to the idea that God will hear and respond to our prayers for our children, protect and guide them from harm, or even bring deliverance from drugs or alcohol... which I believe are demonic instruments of Satan, over which God has given believers authority *(Luke 10:19).*

Some also look to Paul's words shared with a Philippian jailer, as encouragement that God will work in the lives of our family and bring them into a relationship with Christ. Paul said, *"Believe on the Lord Jesus Christ, and you will be saved, you and your household" (Acts 16:31).* While this more likely refers to household members who also believe, it is nonetheless encourages the confidence that the faith and prayers of parents do retain a special influence on their children. Also, I tend to believe that the presence of the Holy Spirit in the heart of a passionate believing parent, as well as in their home environment, can be felt and impact all the members of that household.

When a child grows up, leaves the home and develops a mind of their own, it obviously becomes more challenging to wield the same weight of spiritual influence. This is why it is crucial to influence a child toward the things of God while they are still in the home, young and impressionable. The word of God encourages, *"Train up a child in the way he should go, And when he is old he will not depart from it" (Proverbs 22:6).*

However, while God will not force anyone to do anything against their will, we can offer fervent prayers for God to deal with our child's heart and will. We should stand on the premise of scripture for the Lord to save our household, to bring our children back to the paths of Christ. And we should exercise faith and spiritual authority against demonic powers seeking to manipulate their lives.

61. Can Prayer Help Me Get Even with My Enemies?

Prayer is not merely a weapon or tool to serve your purposes. Prayer is a holy act of communion with your Heavenly Father... intended to bring you into harmony with His desires and His will. Be assured, God will not be manipulated to carry out your whims to even a score, or to take your side against another. God is the fair and righteous judge of the universe.

However, as God's children, we are entitled to ask Him to intervene in our affairs, to protect us, or to bring about justice to unjust situations, such as when people have done evil things against us. This was the whole focus of Jesus' parable of the widow who kept nagging the earthly judge to avenge her of her adversary. *"And shall God not avenge His own elect who cry out day and night to Him, though He bears long with them?" (Luke 18:7).*

The important thing for you is to not seek revenge, but to take such matters to the Lord in prayer, and give Him your wounds of injustice, unfairness or betrayal. Ask Him for His help and intervention in the matter... and to replace your anger with His peace. Let Him be the one to judge the motives and actions of those who have done you wrong... to determine what retribution if any is warranted to bring against them. *"Dear friends, never take revenge. Leave that to the righteous anger of God. For the Scriptures say, 'I will take revenge; I will pay them back,' says the Lord" (Romans 12:19 NLT).*

This may help explain "why" not all prayers are answered... at least in the way that some often wanted them answered. Otherwise, I think that in anger, many believers would probably make presumptuous judgments, and quickly call fire down from Heaven to dispense swift and devastating justice *(Luke 9:54)*. Fortunately for all of us, *"The Lord is merciful and gracious, Slow to anger, and abounding in mercy" (Psalms 103:8)*.

Eventually in the Lord's time, when He feels His mercy and patience has run its course, He will avenge all those who have been abused or mistreated... and fairly judge and punish those who have done evil. Henry Wadsworth Longfellow once wrote, *"Though the mills of God grind slowly, yet they grind exceeding small; Though with patience He stands waiting, With exactness grinds He all."*

And what a terrible and dreadful thing to be on the opposing side of God's justice. Though His mercy and grace are infinite, His judgments and vengeance are equally severe and thorough. *"For we know Him who said, 'Vengeance is Mine, I will repay,' says the Lord. And again, The Lord will judge His people. It is a fearful thing to fall into the hands of the living God" (Hebrews 10:30-31)*.

Meanwhile, take hold of the attitude of Jesus... not by hoping for the downfall and destruction of your enemy, but for their repentance and redemption. Pray for your enemies, so that they will repent for their evil. But also, so that you can release your animosity and forgive them, so you can live in peace.

Holding on to a grudge or bitterness, doesn't hurt anyone but you, by robbing you of joy, and hindering your relationship with God. *"You have heard that it was said, you shall love your neighbor and hate your enemy. But I say to you, love your enemies, bless those who curse you, do good to those who hate you, and pray for those who spitefully use you and persecute you"* *(Matthew 5:43-44).* *(See also Romans 12:19-20)*

One Last Question

I pray that these thoughts about prayer will bring added strength and encouragement to your faith. However, before I conclude, I want to reverse roles for a moment, and be the one to ask one last important question: **"Do you know for sure that you're saved, and that you would go to heaven should you die today?"**

I'm not asking whether you go to church, or if you believe that there is a God... but **"Do you know Jesus in a real and personal way? Have you received Him into your heart as your personal Savior and Lord?"**

If your answer is anything but an absolute YES, I ask you to make this the moment to remove all doubts, to put your faith in Jesus Christ, and accept the free gift of His salvation and eternal life that he offers you.

How to Become a Christian

The most important thing to realize is that God loves you and wants to save you and have fellowship with you, but there's something that separates you from God... sin.

Sin is often thought of as some vile or immoral act, but the Bible helps us understand that it is much more... it is actually an attitude of rebellion against the ideals of God, intrinsic to our inherited human nature. In other words, it is the nature for all human beings to think, do or say things that violate God's holy standards.

According to scripture, this is a condition that was passed down to all the ancestors of Adam, the first man... who allowed sin to alienate himself from God's presence, and which continues to obstruct man's fellowship from the Lord today. The Bible says, ***"For all have sinned and fall short of the glory of God" (Romans 3:23).***

Not only does sin separate us from God in our present time, but it also maintains that separation beyond the grave... in a dreadful realm of eternal death and darkness that was never intended for mankind. The Bible says that the Lake of Fire was created as a place of everlasting punishment for the Devil and his angels, who sinned and rebelled against God, and were expelled from Heaven long ago.

Unfortunately, this hellish place will also be the shared destination of all those who remain separated from God when they face death. ***"And anyone not found written in the Book of Life was cast into the lake of fire" (Revelation 20:15).***

However, the great news is, rather than to abandon the fallen sinful human creatures that God originally created for His fellowship, God loved mankind so much that He devised a plan to redeem us, giving everyone an opportunity to make a choice... either to continue in sin and apart from God... or to turn to the Lord, receive His offer of forgiveness and walk in His fellowship. A relationship with the Lord brings new spiritual life and assurance of everlasting life with the Lord in Heaven when we die.

To implement His plan for redemption, however, God also had to find a way to comply with His own righteous standards by fulfilling His law of sin and death. In other words, according to God's values, death is an irrevocable consequence of sin that must be satisfied. So, in order to rescue man from death without violating His own principles, He found an alternate means to fulfill the demands of His law. He sent His son, Jesus, to die in our place. *"For the wages of sin is death, but the gift of God is eternal life in Christ Jesus our Lord" (Romans 6:23).*

The only sacrifice acceptable to fulfill this enormous debt in behalf of every man, woman and child on the earth, required a perfect, sinless sacrifice. Jesus, the son of God, was the only one who could take our place, since He is the only man without sin to ever walk on the earth.

So, God makes this amazing offer of forgiveness and salvation available as a free gift to every person, if they will comply with just one thing: To believe on the Lord Jesus Christ. *"For God so loved the world that He gave His only begotten Son, that whoever believes in Him should not perish but have everlasting life" (John 3:16).*

To believe on Him means that by faith we accept that Jesus was indeed God's son, who came and died in our behalf on the cross, rose from the dead on the third day, and was exalted by the Heavenly Father as both our Savior and Lord.

The instant you acknowledge this reality in your heart and confess Jesus as your Lord and Savior, something extraordinary occurs... in fact, it is miraculous. The Spirit of Christ is born in your heart and you become a habitation of the Lord's presence. Becoming born-again

225

brings new spiritual life, and God's promise of salvation
and everlasting life. The Lord receives you as His child,
and writes your name in the Lamb's Book of Life.
"Rejoice because your names are written in heaven"
(Luke 10:20).

So, are you ready to accept this gift of salvation that Jesus
offers you right now? The scripture says, *"If you confess*
with your mouth the Lord Jesus and believe in your
heart that God has raised Him from the dead, you
will be saved. For with the heart one believes unto
righteousness, and with the mouth confession is
made unto salvation" (Romans 10:9-10).

Here's a sample prayer that you can put into your
own words:

"Dear Lord Jesus, I realize that I am a sinner and
that I need of your forgiveness. I believe that you
died for my sins on the cross and rose from the dead
so you could wash me of sin and give me eternal life.
Please come into my heart now, forgive me and save
me. I confess you as my Lord and Savior and place
my faith in you. I will follow you as long as I live,
and trust that when I die, you will receive me into
Heaven. Thank you for your forgiveness, for coming
into my heart, for making me a child of God!"

The very moment you sincerely express this prayer to
Christ in faith, He will enter your heart by His Spirit. You
may or may "not" feel or sense anything different at
first... but don't be too concerned with that right now. For
the moment, simply trust in His promise by faith. Jesus
promised to save you, to forgive "all" your sins, and to

write your name in His book of Life... at the very instant you call out for the Lord to come into your heart! And as you continue to walk in your new faith in Christ, you will begin to sense a growing awareness His inner peace, joy and presence along with other encouraging things in the days and weeks ahead.

After this, it's important to start reading the Bible each day to see what God has to say to you (start in the New Testament book of John) ... and is equally important to talk to Him daily through prayer. Ask Him to guide your life and to fill you with the fullness of His Holy Spirit.

Be sure to get involved with a good Bible-believing church and attend faithfully. Ask to be baptized in water at your earliest convenience, in obedience to what Lord commanded *(Acts 2:38)*, and by all means continue to live your life daily for the Lord!

If this book has inspired your life in Christ, please let us know. Contact us at www.victorious.org.

93652030R00128

Made in the USA
Columbia, SC
15 April 2018